EXPLOSIVE GROWTH

EXPLOSIVE GROWTH

A FEW THINGS I LEARNED WHILE GROWING TO

100 MILLION USERS

—AND LOSING $78 MILLION

CLIFF LERNER

This book recounts the author's experiences based on his recollections of the many fast-paced events recounted in this book. The views expressed herein are solely those of the author in his personal capacity and do not necessarily reflect the views of any other person or corporate entity. No representation is made as to the accuracy of any names, timelines, dates, statistics, metrics, and any other facts or information presented herein. The advice and strategies contained herein are for informational purposes only and may not be suitable for your situation. The author welcomes any comments from readers and will review any requests for corrections. The book is not intended as an investment guide. It should not be construed as financial advice of any kind. Neither the author nor Clifford Ventures Corporation assumes any responsibility for any loss of profit, errors, omissions or contrary interpretations of the subject matter herein.

CLIFFORD VENTURES CORPORATION

EXPLOSIVE GROWTH

A Few Things I Learned While Growing To 100 Million Users - And Losing $78 Million

ISBN   978-1-61961-769-8 Paperback

978-1-61961-770-4 Ebook

Access more Explosive Growth materials at:

http://www.explosive-growth.com

Social: @ExplosiveGrowthCEO, @CliffLerner,

#ExplosiveGrowthTip

"My father gave me the greatest gift anyone could give another person: he believed in me."

—JIM VALVANO, HEAD COACH OF THE NCAA CHAMPIONSHIP MEN'S BASKETBALL TEAM, NORTH CAROLINA STATE UNIVERSITY WOLFPACK

This book is dedicated to Mom and Dad. Without their contributions, support, and belief in me, none of this would have been possible.

CONTENTS

ACKNOWLEDGMENTS

I first want to thank the entire team at Book In A Box. Specifically, Tucker Max and Zack Obront for convincing me to write this book, and Hal Clifford, Kathleen Pedersen, and especially David Caissie for making it all possible with their tireless contributions.

A special thanks to my brother, Darrell Lerner, who was instrumental as he spent countless hours helping me copywrite, edit, proofread, and much more.

However, mostly I want to acknowledge all the employees, investors, friends, PR folks, advisors, consultants, lawyers, and many others who put their faith in me and took a chance on SNAP, and for each of you I'm so grateful.

Here's just a few of them who helped make this all possible:

Abby Ross, Adam Caplan, Adam Gries, Adam Handelsman, Adam Purvis, Aegis Capital Corp, Alan Cost, Alan Tepper, Alexander Harrington, Ali Bennett, Alicia Raymond, Alina Libova, Ana Berman, Ana Ledesma, Andrew Metersky, Andrew Weinreich, Arash Vakil, Arianne Perry, Aric Jacover, Arnie Owen, Ashek Ahmed, Ashley Williams, Benjamin Perroud, Botond Denes, Brian Balfour, Briana Amato, Brooke Hamilton, Bryan Packman, Byron Lerner, Caitlin McCabe, Caterina Correa, Cesar Bodden, Chris Mirabile, Chris Outram, Chrissy Fleming, Christina Metaxas, Christofer Nystrom, Christopher Jenkins, Christopher Mika, Craig Schwabe, Cyriel DiKoume, Dan Kohn, Daniel Chapsky, Daniel Fasulo, Daniel Straus, Daniel Wharton, Darrell Lerner, David Bocchi, David Caissie, David Evans, David Fox, David Perry, David Raphael, David & Kelly Hantman, Derek Webb, Devashish Kandpal, Devin Cooper, Dirk Heikoop, Dmitry Moskalenko, Doug Lin, Edwin Iskandar, Ehud Cohen, Elena Shulman, Elisabeth Murphy, Emily Joyce, Eric Sackowitz, Eric Tjaden, Erty Seidel, Frank Jackson, Gary Burke, Gavin Castro, Geoff Brookins, Grace Paik, Greg Frantz, Greg Kramer, Greg Samuel, Gregg Jaclin, Hal Clifford, Hayden Vestal, Haynes and Boone, Helen Trieu, Howard Katzenberg, James Murdica, James Supple, Jamie Fraser, Janna Biagio, Jason Dove, Jason Katz, Jason Kimler, Jason Markowitz, Jason McCreary, Jason Zwick, Jayson Gaignard, Jeff Cohen, Jeff Rosenthal, Jen Gilbert, Jenna Freed, Jennifer Bassiur, Jennifer Litt, Jennifer Wisinski, Jenny Lerner, Jeremy Pippin, Jerry King, Jessica Tubbs, Jimmy Tubbs, Joanna Barber, Joe Jaigobind, Joel Miele, Jon Guido, Jon Pedersen, Jonathan Zaback, Joseph Austin, Joseph Russell, Josh Elman, Joshua Fischer, Judy Krandel, Justin Medoy, Justin Roman, Kathleen Pedersen, Katie Lambert, Kayla Inserra, Kelly Burke, Keren Lerner, Kevin Liu, Kimberly Bouton, Kristen Tubbs, Laura O'Donnell, Lauren Bishop, Lauren Urasek, Leah Taylor, Lee Linden, Lisa Chin, Lisa Dubrow, Lonnie Rosenbaum, Lynn Simon, Lynne Lerner, Lyuba Shipovich, Mackenzie Mills, Mallory Prahalis, Man Hoang, Marc Perry, Maria Seredina, Mark Brooks, Mark Lesnic, Matt Barr, Matt Fry, Matthew Sadofsky, Mel and Linda Bernstein, Mel Tanenbaum, Melissa Tubbs, Michael Barany, Michael Dill, Michael Hartman, Michael Jones, Michael Petrovich, Michael Pritchard, Michael Sherov, Michael Worthington, Michelle Levine, Miguel Molinari, Mrudula Chakravarthy, Nazar Ivaniv, Neil Foster, Nicholas Disanto, Nick O'Neill, Nicole Hendrickson, Nicole Larsen, Olivia Lin, Patrick Leary, Paul Cardillo, Paul Marino, Paul Wieckiewicz, Peter Cho, Phil Cardillo, Randi Kendler, Rashan Jibowu, Rebecca Iannaccone, Rianna Billington, Richard Anslow, Richard Howard, Rick Werner, Robert Brisita, Russ Kuchman, Ryan Faber, Samuel Goodwin, Sarah McClitis, Sarah Meyer, Sean C.

Cooley, Seth Godin, Shadi Garman, Sheldon Shalom, Sigma Capital, Stephanie Bhonslay, Steven Fox, Steven Surowiec, Susan Threadgill, Susan Wetzel, Tai Lopez, Taj Corinaldi, Tanoy Sinha, Teddy Lo, Thomas Carrella, Tim Rogus, Tom O'Shea, Tucker Max, Wei Kin Huang, William Leach, Wilmary Soto-Guignet, Yoonjin Lee, Zack Obront.

FOREWORD

BY DARRELL LERNER

Imagine waking up one morning to find your previously unknown start-up all over the news. After years of hard work and unsuccessful investor pitches, your valuation has increased tenfold overnight and investors are suddenly acknowledging your success and banging down your door to throw money at you. Within a few weeks, you've raised nearly $10 million on the basis of just a few phone calls, and every media outlet in the world wants to talk to you. Sounds like something out of a dream or a movie, right? Well, this crazy story is entirely true. As SNAP Interactive's cofounder and Cliff's brother, I was fortunate enough to be there for nearly all of it.

Sometimes you meet someone and you can immediately tell how smart they are. Cliff Lerner is one of those people—he's a genius. His thinking is on a whole different level, and I would back his analytical skills against anyone.

When Facebook launched its app platform in 2007, it offered free access to hundreds of millions of users for those smart enough to figure out the right mix of marketing, engagement, and analytics—someone like Cliff. As a result of Cliff's analytical background, he took to the new Facebook platform like a fish to water. He executed a near-perfect blend of testing, optimization, and viral techniques that resulted in millions of users for our product in short order, and a business whose growth outpaced what we were prepared to handle.

As a result of that explosive growth, Cliff faced numerous challenges and made a few inevitable mistakes. That's also how he lost $78 million, and that's what makes this story so compelling.

Explosive Growth isn't about an uninterrupted rise to success, and it isn't a book that simply lists a bunch of growth strategies without context or practical application—anyone can do that. The marketing strategies, PR hacks, and viral expertise that helped us accumulate 100 million users are all in here. But what's perhaps more valuable are the lessons learned from hard times and a real-time window into the decision making as things were exploding.

Success in business doesn't come from an idea or a formula; it comes from execution. No path is identical, and each key moment presents a decision point that will impact and shape the future of the business. The strategies in this book, coupled with a glimpse into the thought processes behind key decisions in SNAP's journey, will undoubtedly help any entrepreneur better execute in their own business.

When Cliff and I cofounded SNAP Interactive, we were optimistic. But I never could have imagined that several years later, we'd be ringing the opening bell at NASDAQ, have our office profiled in Business Insider, or be recognized during a family dinner at Peter Lugers (the top New York steakhouse) as "the computer kids we just read about in the newspaper."

Cliff's story is absolutely incredible! I know it, because I lived it.

—DARRELL LERNER, CO-FOUNDER OF SNAP INTERACTIVE, FOUNDER OF ALLPAWS.COM

INTRODUCTION

"Make your life a story worth telling."

—ADAM BRAUN, FOUNDER OF PENCILS OF PROMISE

It was December 22, 2010, and most corporate office environments were likely recovering from some sort of massive holiday party blowout—the kind where a few too many drinks were consumed, a few too many inappropriate things were said, and way too many regrets were felt. That wasn't the case at the corporate office for my company, SNAP Interactive, creators of the online dating app, AreYouInterested? (AYI). We had other things on our minds.

I forget exactly what time of the day it was when I got the

call from Bloomberg News, but I do have a fairly vivid recollection of how it all went down.

As soon as I picked up the phone, the reporter abruptly asked me, "I have one quick question for you guys. This might sound strange, but do you guys work out of someone's garage?"

I was caught a little off guard by the bizarre nature of such a question from out of nowhere. "Of course not," I explained. "You were in our office a couple months ago on 30th Street and 7th Avenue in New York City." I elaborated for him, "You asked for open access to our employees and to check out our data sources, because you wanted to verify information for a potential story. While you were here, you also said we might be the best undiscovered public company out there."

The reporter acknowledged my explanation, and verified the facts with me one more time. "Okay, I just wanted to make sure that you didn't move operations to a garage somewhere for some reason."

"No, we definitely didn't do that. Why do you ask?"

"Never mind," he assured me. "Just be sure to check out the news tomorrow."

After hearing the click and dial tone, an unsettling mixture of emotions followed—curiosity, anticipation, and more than a little nervous tension.

DECEMBER 23

When I woke up the next morning and checked out the news online, I noticed a very detailed and in-depth news story titled, "Facebook Friends in Search of Romance Drive App Growth" on Bloomberg News.

It was a nice enough piece; the content was very flattering to our company, describing the uniqueness of our product and the advanced metrics we applied to optimally serve our users. However, the most significant aspect of the article was in the following quote from the CEO of IAC (the parent company of Match.com), Gregory R. Blatt:

"AreYouInterested? is a flirty, fun little app. They have a few people working in a garage. We've got hundreds of engineers maximizing our business. You need huge degrees of sophistication, huge amounts of data behind it, and a huge community."

Whether it was a snarky comment to describe our corporate office as a garage, or if he actually thought we operated out of a garage, is still a mystery to me. I suspect he was so out of touch that he actually thought we ran our business from someone's garage. Nonetheless, a big question arose in my mind.

How should I react to an industry leader taking cheap shots at my start-up? I pondered the possibilities:

- Should I be flattered? After all, Apple got started from the garage of Steve Jobs's parents.
- Should I fire back with my own snarky remark about how Match.com is too big to have the necessary pulse of its own user base?
- Should I devise some sort of *Animal House*-style prank for Blatt at their corporate office? (However, I didn't see a John Belushi-type in our office who would be capable or even remotely interested in executing such a pointless task.)
- Or, should I offer my undying gratitude?

Gratitude might seem like an unusual reaction, but it was ultimately what I chose, and it proved appropriate given the next sequence of events.

Whatever the reason for Blatt's comment, the important thing was that AYI had obviously arrived. A surefire sign that the industry leader is concerned with your presence is when they dismiss you with a not-so-subtle dig like the one in this article.

Before the article came out, our stock was a very illiquid penny stock, which traded zero shares the previous day. That's right—zero—as in, no trading at all. By the time the closing bell rang on December 23, the stock had shot up from $0.20 to $0.50 per share. That's a nice little bump—especially when it was likely fueled by one article containing one innocuous comment—certainly worthy of notice, but the best was yet to come.

DECEMBER 24 (CHRISTMAS EVE)

The following day was Christmas Eve, so the markets were closed and there wasn't a lot of news breaking. With little else to report on, our story simmered in the news pot for a while longer. It was published in some other big-time media outlets, like the *L.A. Times*. It's tough to imagine so little going on in the city of L.A. that an article about a small tech company thousands of miles away would be considered worthy of publication, but that's exactly what happened. The snowball effect had officially begun.

DECEMBER 26

Christmas was on a Saturday that year, so December 26 fell on a Sunday. That timing meant the stock market had been closed for three days since the article featuring AYI had come out. This was the business version of the perfect storm: a seriously buzzworthy news article sticking around and creating a rising hot stock, and nowhere for either one to go because of the holiday break.

DECEMBER 27

I showed up for work on Monday, December 27 just like any other day, except that day there was a note on my desk that Maria Bartiromo, the lead financial news anchor at CNBC had called (also known as the "Money Honey") and she wanted a callback ASAP.

At first, I wasn't sure if the message was real or some sort of unfunny practical joke, because financial news didn't get any bigger than Maria Bartiromo. Sure enough, it was the real deal. After turning on the television and reading some online articles from around the country, I discovered that AYI was a lead story on the news that day. Before the closing bell, our stock had soared to unimaginable heights of around $1.50 per share. We went from zero shares traded two days previously and ten days out of the previous thirteen, to trading 2,495,000 shares in one day! What could be next?

DECEMBER 28

The snowball effect was gaining momentum. We were getting television coverage from sources all over the country. Henry Blodget, a prominent former Wall Street analyst and founder of Business Insider, came out with a story about us on December 28. He said that he hadn't had the chance to do his homework on us yet, but the numbers looked very promising. AYI had become so hot that even though he knew nothing about us, he still had to mention us or risk appearing out of touch. That led to even more television coverage from Bloomberg and CNBC.

DECEMBER 29

On December 29—not even one week from the day we got a mysterious phone call asking if we worked out of someone's garage—our stock traded 3.6 million shares and was up over 1,500 percent! Time to take a victory lap, right? Not the way I looked at it, which is why another big question arose in my mind.

What should I do as the cofounder of a start-up whose stock price had gone up exponentially high overnight? Once again, I pondered the possibilities:

- 💣 Should I pop a $500 bottle of champagne and call Justin Bieber to get on a celebrity cruise right away?
- 💣 Should I visit my most disliked teacher from high school and rub a wad of hundred-dollar bills in his face?

💣 Maybe I should stop by an ex-girlfriend's house in a blazing red Ferrari with a girl who looked like Sofia Vergara's younger, hotter sister.

💣 Or, should I just say, "Huh, how 'bout that?" and experience an overwhelming sense of concern about what this means for the more long-lasting success of my organization?

Counter-intuitive as this may seem, my reaction was not one of unfettered joy or glorious celebration. For me, it was natural to be concerned about the company and the people who helped me build it. I was worried about our ability to remain focused.

In other words, no call to *The Biebs* was ever made.

There also wasn't any rubbing of money in an overworked, over-matched high school teacher's face.

And most regrettably, no younger, hotter version of Sofia Vergara was ever paraded *Fast and Furious*-style in a luxury Italian sports car through the streets of my hometown.

I was legitimately concerned that these ten to twelve extremely talented and hard-working people—so valuable to our success, who shared my unbridled enthusiasm for building a great product from the ground up—would get distracted.

I was worried that our drive to innovate would diminish, that we would stop out-working other companies, and ultimately that we would lose our way as an organization. For a short while, it was utter madness in the garage at 30th and 7th.

People had one eye on their work and another on the stock ticker. Who could blame them? Because most of them were paid largely from stock, several of them were officially paper millionaires—scratch that—paper *multi-millionaires*. We had become the number one story on Wall Street. It got so crazy that I had to totally ban watching CNBC and all financial websites at work.

It turns out that getting to this point was the easy part. What followed was an emotional and professional roller coaster ride, enough to test the mental fortitude of the Dalai Lama during a three-week-long meditation bender and mindfulness blowout.

Opportunities were seized, regrets were had, and success was ultimately achieved. But most significantly, some infinitely invaluable lessons were learned all along the way that will serve me well going forward, and I'd like to share them with you.

1

MY EPIPHANY AT
LEHMAN BROTHERS

"In the end, it's not the things we did that we regret, it's the things we didn't do."

—UNKNOWN

I graduated from Cornell University in the year 2000 with a degree in Applied Economics and Business Management. Fresh out of my program, I was presented with an opportunity to work in a brand new group in the equities division at Lehman Brothers—the hottest investment bank in the country at the time. Everyone wanted a job there. On the surface, this seemed like a big break for a kid just graduating college and trying to find his way in the corporate world.

Lehman Brothers wanted me to start immediately. Perfect, right? Not for me; I had planned a two-week trip to Europe with my friends after graduation. I was really looking forward to this once-in-a-lifetime opportunity to see the world, experience different cultures, and visit breathtaking locales. So, full of Ivy League confidence and naive optimism, I asked Lehman Brothers if I could have a two-week break between graduation and my start date. It seemed like an easy enough request to grant, because every other new hire in the analyst training program wasn't going to start for another month anyway.

Unfortunately, Lehman Brothers didn't see it the same way. They said something like, "You need to be here tomorrow or we're giving your job to someone else." The problem was that they had just created a brand new department with only one person in it so far, and they thought I was a perfect fit to complement him. They wanted me there right away. Suddenly, that Ivy League confidence and naive optimism was replaced with professional bitterness and forlorn disenchantment.

EIGHT-HUNDRED PAGES THAT DEFINITELY COULD HAVE WAITED

Initially, I figured I was going to Europe anyway, but my parents set me straight on that pretty quickly. A bit humbled, but entirely ready to put it all behind me, I showed up for work on day one just as they asked. When I got there, however, I had no chair to sit in, no desk to work at, and no computer to login to. The bitterness and disenchantment quickly resumed and intensified.

Fortunately, they got me a chair rather quickly, but the computer and the desk took about two weeks. Really? Could I not have been carefully searching the streets of Rome for the best trattoria in the world, or experiencing the majestic beauty of the Eiffel Tower in Paris, during those weeks? Instead, I was told to read the 800-page manual for Microsoft Excel, word-for-word until they set up a computer for me. They must have known it was going to take a while to get me situated.

Although I was understandably a little perturbed at the inflexibility of my start date, I soldiered on and made the best of my early time in that group. I grew to become grateful for that slow ramp-up, because being able to make Excel sing, and learning the ins and outs of the business served me well going forward. In fact, I garnered a reputation for being a whiz at Excel, which helped me to automate tasks that previously took hours, and that ability helped me stand out from the pack. So, I suppose it ended up being a worthwhile two weeks after all.

I was part of the product management group, and my responsibilities included supporting all the senior product managers, pitching my own trading ideas, and running the afternoon research call, which I actually loved doing. I got to talk to different analysts from many different industries while learning and observing what made certain companies perform well for several years while others underwhelmed. That turned out to be a great fit for me, because a long time ago, my grandfather was a very prominent presence on Wall Street, and he even had Warren Buffet subscribe to his investment service. When I was much younger, he got me started in stock trading. It would have been an even better fit if it had started two weeks later, but that was all in the past. Or, was it?

SAD SCENES

In 2005, Lehman Brothers promoted me to a very prominent role, where I would run the morning research call as well as the afternoon one. Because the morning research call was televised to all the bank branches throughout the organization, my position was the most visible one in the entire firm. The problem with that visibility was that it was a lot like being a doctor on-call. I had to keep my eyes on the breaking news all night to know which stocks needed to be discussed during the next morning's call. Therefore, not only was I at work at 5:30 every morning to get a jump on things, but I was also on-call throughout the night.

Although I enjoyed the job a lot and liked the people around me, this wasn't the kind of lifestyle that a twenty-seven-year-old bachelor in New York considered ideal. The metaphorical sand that got kicked in my face came from living across the street from a popular nightclub on 13th Street and 4th Avenue. I remember battling the club goers there at 5:00 every morning for a taxi; except they were fighting—rather vociferously, from moderate inebriation and God only knows what else—for a cab to go home in, and I was fighting—rather dejectedly from moderate depression (not clinically, but you get the point)—for a cab to go to work in.

Another sad scene I remember was going on dates and looking at my watch around 8:30 to 9:00 at night and saying, "All right, (yawn) it's been fun, but I have to get to bed now, because I need to be up in a few hours." Of course, contributing to this emotional turmoil was the fact that I was still a junior employee, and perhaps a little more bitter than I initially realized about not getting my trip to Europe.

Clearly, what I was doing wasn't satisfying my inherent drive to innovate, my passion for making a difference in the world, and my love for travel. Inspiration comes from strange places sometimes. For me, it came from watching the cult classic and comic masterpiece *Office Space*, one fateful night. If you haven't seen it, *Office Space* is a brilliant movie from the late 90s about soul-sucking corporate office culture.

OFFICE SPACE AS INSPIRATION

My epiphany came from the scene in which the lead character, Peter, is talking to his therapist and his wife (who he secretly hates)—although the hatred has much more to do with his job than with her behavior. He says something like, "Ever since the day I started working, every day has been worse than the one before it." Then, the therapist asks him, "What about today? Are you saying today is the worst day of your life?" Peter calmly replies that yes, today is the worst day of his life.

Although I never reached Peter's level of desperation, I found myself drawing way too many parallels between his situation and mine. I wanted to be my own boss, and God knows I wanted to travel. I wasn't getting any younger, and the pressure to change things was mounting every day as I saw the years roll past me. Ultimately, I wanted to control my own destiny, but I needed an idea to make it happen.

At the time, my office location (complete with desk, chair, and computer at this point) was between two attractive females, who, as part of their job, would meet with clients after work to share strategy and stock ideas with salespeople. The women were both single, and I noticed they were also both on Match.com a lot during the day.

When they had client meetings, they showed up for work in their best dresses, ready to impress. However, their client meetings would frequently get cancelled, so they would log on to Match.com and attempt to find dates for the night. Unfortunately, the site's functionality didn't support that. It was a long and tedious process to get an online date in those days. Here's what it usually looked like:

1. Browse a seemingly infinite set of profiles that meet the search criteria.
2. Send an email to someone who seems like a good match.
3. With any luck, a reply to the email is received. This is the online dating equivalent of the Golden Ticket in a Wonka Bar.
4. Over the course of the next several days, a few emails get sent back and forth.
5. If everything goes well, and nobody says anything stupid or shares any inappropriate images (which guys

do far more often than most people realize) a phone
call might be scheduled.

6. A few days later, the phone rings, and after an hour-
long phone conversation to determine similar interests,
a date might be arranged for the following weekend.

It was a long process just to have a cup of coffee or go to
the putt-putt course with someone. All things considered,
the process of getting a date usually lasted several days—
more than likely, a couple of weeks. From this harsh reality
of the industry's shortcomings, the wheels of innovation
began to churn in my head.

PARTING ISN'T ALWAYS SUCH SWEET SORROW

If these two very attractive, smart, professional women
were looking to find dates at the last minute and couldn't,
there had to be an addressable need there. That's when
my idea came to me!

I could build an online dating site that catered to busy
professionals, who didn't have the time to spend days or
weeks emailing back and forth to get a date.

#ExplosiveGrowthTip 1: Find something that people are doing inefficiently and create a solution that makes it substantially easier (ten times easier) to achieve the same result. Does your product accomplish this?

I walked into my boss's office the next morning after my epiphany and told him I was leaving. He started ranting, "Are you crazy? We just offered you a promotion!" I handed him my two-week notice and walked out. He didn't talk to me until my last day, when he completely freaked out on me. "You're fucking serious! You can't actually go! What about showing us some shred of goddamned loyalty?"

For some reason (maybe it was out of fear of his blood pressure hitting upwards of 300 over a million, causing his head to explode in a vicious spray of blood and grey shrapnel), I agreed to stay on for a few more weeks to train some new people for him.

He berated me throughout my extended departure process, incessantly asking why I wanted to leave. I told him I wanted to start a business, but also wanted some time off to travel (big surprise, eh?). After being asked the same question for the umpteenth time, I finally told him I needed six months off before I could even think about working for him again. Truthfully, I thought six months off would give me just enough time to pursue my own business and see how far I got, but I wasn't going to tell him that.

A couple weeks later, it was my last day—again. I said my goodbyes, hugged it out with all my coworkers, cleaned out my desk and was about to leave when he made his last-ditch effort to keep me.

"Fine," he said. "I've spoken to some people, and I'm not letting you leave. Here's a piece of paper. Write down whatever it is you want." I calmly wrote down, "Six months off." I even spelled it out for him in big, plain, easy-to-read letters. Commence freak-out number two. He read it, cursed (rather loudly), and threw his phone against the wall, while screaming at me, "Get the fuck out of here! I had the authority to pay you a lot more money.

I'm personally going to make sure you never work on Wall Street again!"

Alas, that was the end of my tenure at Lehman Brothers, and I never spoke to him again. Shortly thereafter, I was on a plane to Europe, where I vacationed for several weeks.

DOUBLE DOWN

After reaching out to other entrepreneurs and friends, I learned a lot about starting a business. It became clear to me that one of the most common mistakes people make is massively underestimating the amount of money they need to start a business and get traction.

Let's say you think you'll need $100,000 to keep your business afloat for twelve months. What happens if you're not having immediate success just six months into your business's infancy? You're not giving yourself any cushion in that scenario to keep the business afloat in those last six months. You've also got the added pressure of spending that last six months in a balancing act. You're trying to save your business and (potentially) finding your next job at the same time, which makes success in each endeavor that much harder. If you fail at both, you're going to be out on the street.

I didn't want to live with that fear of diverting my attention from the business so quickly, so whatever my estimate was to start operations, I doubled it. Luckily, my experience at Lehman Brothers taught me a lot about the stock market, and I came up with a system of trading stocks to support myself during the early years. It was a simple and automated quantitative-based trading system, but it worked well enough that I didn't have to pay myself any salary for the first three-and-a-half years while I learned the new business.

#ExplosiveGrowthTip 2: Once you've figured out how much start-up capital you need, double it.

#ExplosiveGrowthTip 3: Make the unknown known by creating a worst-case scenario plan. You'll discover that the situation is rarely as bad as you initially thought. Do you have a worst-case scenario plan?

PREPARATION INSTEAD OF PANIC

Fear of the unknown is a destructive force. It causes people to make suboptimal choices by avoiding that fear, rather than wisely preparing for the future. One good way to prepare instead of panicking is to go through every potential problem scenario and write down what action to take if it comes to pass.

In essence, you're living the moment or scenario in your head before it actually takes place. If the event happens, it will still suck, but it's much less scary because you've already imagined it and determined what steps you're going to take. You can remove the panic and just hit the play button on your plan. It's also a great way to avoid constantly waking up at 3:00 a.m. in a cold sweat when times are tough.

My brother Darrell founded and ran a very success-ful company called AllPaws, which I'll discuss in a little more detail later on. At one point, when cash was dwindling, and he didn't know if he'd be able to raise additional capital or find a successful exit for AllPaws, he went through this exercise of preparation.

He made a detailed plan in advance, a list of actions he could take in a doomsday scenario, all the way down to what he'd do in the event if he had only one month of cash remaining. The actions included things like:

- Which companies he would approach to sell the database to

- Which vendors to ask for discounts or free services from

- Which partners he would try to renegotiate revenue share agreements with

He knew the options weren't terribly appealing, but at least the playbook was ready. If the time came, all he had to do was pull it out and execute, instead of being overwhelmed by worry, stress, and depression at a time that required clarity and presence of mind. Having that plan ready in advance made the thought of such a scenario much less scary than simply proclaiming, "Oh, shit! If we don't get any bids soon, we're going to run out of money, and then we're fucked." Thankfully that didn't happen, and Darrell eventually accepted a bid from a leader in the industry to achieve a successful exit with AllPaws.

TAKING THE PATH LESS TRAVELED

My brother Darrell and I cofounded the business, which started out as eTwine Holdings Inc. We were fortunate that our combined skill sets created some advantages for us. Darrell had a solid legal background, and I had the Wall Street experience, which afforded us the ability to go public through a process called self-registration. Very few companies do it, because it's not actually an underwritten IPO—meaning you don't raise significant money from institutions. You still need legal and accounting expertise to pull it off.

We hit the ground running once I got back from Europe: getting the site up and running, acquiring users, and generating revenue. All things considered, it took a total of about five months to go public.

IAMFREETONIGHT.COM (IMFT)

The name of the original website was IAmFreeTonight.com, and the objective was to make getting a date ten times easier than it was on other online dating sites. Users didn't need to send dozens of emails back and forth for several days or weeks to schedule a date. Instead, they answered a few questions about what they wanted to do, when, where, and with whom. Then, they could do a quick search for singles nearby who matched their desired availability and activity.

After users answered those few basic questions, we also sent them emails containing the profiles of people with similar interests and availability in the hopes of facilitating a date much quicker than any other platform. For example, I could say that I'm free this coming Saturday night, and I want to see live music at 8:00 p.m. with a woman who is somewhere between twenty-five to thirty-five years old and lives in Manhattan. Once I input that criteria into the system, the emails with profiles of potential matches for that date would flow to my email inbox.

Confidence in the product was never a problem for me. I had a pretty good feeling our product was unique enough to be a hit, due to our key differentiator of indicating when users were free to go on dates. After all, the main value proposition of a dating site was helping singles find dates, so if we could do that ten times faster than other sites, I thought we'd have a hit.

THE FEAR FACTOR AND EMBARRASSMENT STIGMA OF ONLINE DATING

This was 2006, and online dating was still a new concept with a lot of undiscovered territory to explore. There was a lot of growth in the industry, but there were also a lot of issues that presented big roadblocks. The two biggest were fear and embarrassment.

Due to safety concerns, people were terrified to meet strangers they only knew from a website. And since the whole online dating industry was seen as a little taboo, the embarrassment factor was high—nobody wanted to admit to online dating.

The safety concerns were completely irrational to me, because when people meet someone at a bar the old-fashioned way (without introducing themselves online first), they're still meeting a total stranger. At least online dating includes a digital footprint, such as an IP address and email address. When people meet randomly at bars, there's no way to track who they are.

Maybe it was similar to today's public perception of ride-sharing drivers. Today, the media constantly throws stories at us about Uber or Lyft drivers who are not only wanted criminals in fifteen states, but also enjoy kicking puppies in their spare time. The truth is that there are probably just as many unsavory cab drivers in the world as there are Uber or Lyft drivers, potentially many more.

The alleged connection between ride sharing and physical violence doesn't make any sense. Likewise, the paranoia and the negative public perception associated with online dating didn't make any sense to me, but that didn't matter—it was still a problem that we had to address. That's when we introduced a new feature to battle the fear factor of online dating, which was called the "wingman."

THE WINGMAN

The way the wingman feature worked was that the user added friends to their profile as the wingman or wingwoman, indicating they wanted to meet other singles as a group, and then they could search for other groups to go on a date. It was a simple idea, but it served well to alleviate one of the biggest pain points associated with online dating—fear—because there is safety in numbers. The wingman idea was a naturally viral feature since people needed to incorporate friends (who had to get an account) in order to get value out of it.

Match.com and Yahoo! Personals were the two largest dating sites at that point, but there wasn't anything unique about them. As a start-up, I knew we didn't have a lot of capital to work with, but we needed a way to grow quicker, so we implemented a unique feature to inspire that growth. With the wingman feature, we were the first company to meaningfully address the perceived danger of online dating, a very hot topic at the time.

Shortly after its introduction, the wingman idea began to get us some big-time press. There was a feature story in *USA Today* about us, an appearance on Mike and Juliet, (a popular morning show) and even an appearance on the Geraldo TV show, which was also extremely popular at the time. Geraldo's producers found the concept of our dating site to be an interesting fit for business people who were traveling, lonely, and looking for love. So, they filmed the whole show in Union Square in New York City, and for their angle, they said we gave new meaning to the term, "layover." It wasn't quite the concept we were looking for, but it was still major publicity.

Although we did experience some success with the wingman concept and got a lot of media attention, the feature ultimately didn't achieve the explosive viral growth we were hoping for. Since the feature required users to invite their friends, it forced users to reveal they were using an online dating site, which most people just weren't ready for due to the embarrassment factor of online dating at that time.

TINDER SOCIAL AKA THE WINGMAN 2.0

Ten years after we implemented the wingman concept, Tinder introduced "Tinder Social" with success. It was a feature that was just about identical to the wingman concept, where users can switch back and forth between original Tinder mode (one person seeking another) to Social mode, where groups of friends can search for other groups of friends nearby to meet up with. It's an outstanding idea—wish I'd thought of it. Oh, wait a second, I did! Timing—not necessarily being first—is truly everything.

 #ExplosiveGrowthTip 4: First-mover advantage is useless if the timing isn't right. Have you thought about ideas, products, or features that failed in the past—simply due to being too early—that may work now?

MANHATTAN'S GOT TALENT

"Amazing people become increasingly amazing over time."

—JAYSON GAIGNARD, FOUNDER OF MASTERMINDTALKS

How did we come up with unique concepts like the wingman and getting a date within minutes instead of days or weeks? The answer is talent. My brother and I performed well in our respective roles, but some of our early hires played key roles in rapidly growing our business in those formative years.

One such hire was a friend named Jim Supple, who had a prominent job on Wall Street, but he was also very entrepreneurial and knew my family from previous business opportunities. Most importantly, he believed in us and was willing to work entirely for stock at the outset—because we couldn't have afforded him otherwise.

Jim was instrumental in our early success. Not only did Jim provide us with his own keen insight and expertise, but he did a little of everything. Although Jim was hired to lead our finance department, no task was ever "beneath" him if it helped the company and saved a few dollars. He even moved furniture and painted the walls. His hard work was crucial to a young business with little money to spend, and his positive attitude and work ethic set a tone and inspired the young and growing team.

Before we could start getting users and making money, we needed a developer who could take our specs, build a demo for us, and get the site up and running. We got some referrals and went with a firm that built websites, and they assigned a developer to our project. I remember the firm operated out of the basement of an old pasta factory, which was odd, but it worked out—not right away—but, eventually.

For whatever reason, there were numerous delays with our demo—we kept being told they were working on it. Naturally, we got a little anxious, but after three to four months, we finally got to see a demo, which was very exciting.

Finally, after all our careful planning, thoughtful execution, and serious investment of time and money, we had the chance to see what our website would look like—and they showed us someone logging in and logging out. That was it. It took them three to four months to show us how to log in and log out—nothing else. The login/logout experience was so good though, that they even demoed it for us a second time! So, we did what any thoughtful, forward-thinking entrepreneurial group would do at a time like that—we panicked.

We had a talk with the firm about our expectations, because frankly, we didn't know if that was a good demo or not. We knew, however, if that was good, we were screwed. Fortunately, they came back to us and said, "Wait, we have someone who we think is much better." That's when they gave us a hidden gem—Mike Sherov, who single-handedly built IAmFreeTonight.com and later our first Facebook App. Mike was a key hire, playing an irreplaceable role for us in many ways. He eventually joined us full-time, and became our lead developer and head of technology. He stayed with us for another seven or eight years afterward.

Mike saved the day. If it weren't for his leadership and development expertise, who knows what would have happened to the company at such a critical juncture? Team is everything, but a few extremely talented members of that team can make all the difference in the world. If you're a sports fan, think about some of the following analogies:

- How good would the '95-'96 Chicago Bulls have fared without Michael Jordan and Scottie Pippen?
- Would the New England Patriots have won five Super Bowls from 2001-2017 without Bill Belichick and Tom Brady?
- What about the Edmonton Oilers of the 1980s without players like Mark Messier, Paul Coffey, and of course, Wayne Gretzky?

A great team can take you a long way, but elite individual talent might be what you need to get over the hump. I'm not sure if any of the amazing things that happened later would have ever occurred if Jim and Mike weren't onboard in those early days. In fact, I'm almost certain they wouldn't have.

#ExplosiveGrowthTip 5: Your first few hires will set the tone for your culture. Secure elite talent ASAP and hire carefully. Are you confident your last few hires are the right cultural fit?

2

THE EARLY LESSONS LEARNED FROM IAMFREETONIGHT.COM

"I've learned it doesn't matter how many times you've failed, you only have to be right once."

—MARK CUBAN, AMERICAN BUSINESSMAN, INVESTOR, AUTHOR, AND TELEVISION PERSONALITY

Fueled by the hard work of a few integral people, IMFT was up and running in November of 2006. We got our first users and grew at a decent pace considering our limited funds, but I still had a lot to learn.

THE NETWORK EFFECT

One thing we realized after accumulating a user base was the value of the network effect in online dating—a product becomes more valuable when more people use it. For example, when a female from NYC signs up on a dating site, that's a new search result and potential connection for many other users. Imagine Facebook, LinkedIn, or other social networking sites with only a couple of your friends in the user base—it wouldn't be very useful.

The network effect is even more crucial for a dating site, as users only get value if there are thousands of other users they can interact with. Whenever a guy or girl signed up for IAmFreeTonight.com, that's a new profile for users to check out and possibly get a date out of.

The network effect also affects the longevity of an online dating site. If the user base of an online dating site never grows, and all the profiles that are on it are the same ones that were on it six months ago, nobody gets any value out of that, because all possible matches have already been made. Then, there's no reason for anyone to continue using the site.

I realized that all my great ideas about uniqueness weren't going to matter if I didn't find a way to get a large number of users to sign up. I needed to spark interest, create buzz, and get a lot of activity going. We didn't just need a few thousand users—we needed a hundred times that or more. The embarrassment factor of online dating at the time made this seem like an impossible task.

The reason an online dating site needs so many active users to succeed is that if it has 100,000 users spread out equally in the U.S., the most basic search of just an age range, gender, and location will leave most users with less than a hundred profiles to browse. When more detailed search criteria like height, body type, and ethnicity get added, that number is likely reduced to just a few. This issue isn't understood by entrepreneurs starting a dating site, because they drastically underestimate how many active users they need for the site to continuously add value to the user.

This is also why there is rarely a change in the market leaders of products. It's usually a winner-take-all outcome in each niche market, and it's why Match.com, eHarmony, PlentyOfFish.com, Jdate, etc. have been the leaders in their target markets for more than ten years now. Even though there are start-ups every day launching with new, exciting, and even superior features, they rarely gain traction, because the power of the network effect and the winner-take-all outcome is nearly impossible to displace.

We successfully executed the wingman concept to battle

the safety concern with online dating, but the embarrassment factor still lingered, and the question became: how to grow the website in an industry where people don't talk about using it. From that question, we learned a lot of valuable lessons about marketing and revenue growth.

THE $50,000 BUST

An experienced nightclub promoter once pitched a unique way for us to get a flood of new users on the site. It would cost us $50,000 on a spring break promotion. We went all in on that idea, because marketing our product to thousands of users in our core demographic at once seemed like a great way to get the surge of activity we desperately needed.

Helicopters would fly overhead at Key West, and they would drop flyers over the crowd and write "IAmFreeTonight.com" in the sky. Girls in bikinis would walk around handing out flyers all over the place.

It was a massive effort—a marketing blitz to gain an exponential number of users from one big promotion—and it produced a whopping zero signups. That's right, the ROI on our investment was zero users for $50,000. It doesn't take a degree from Cornell to figure out that was not how we wanted to continue to invest our money.

#ExplosiveGrowthTip 6: Learn how to validate an idea with as little time and financial investment as possible. Do you have a plan to validate your ideas cheaply?

BOOK RECOMMENDATIONS

Throughout the book, you'll find several book recommendations that were integral to my success, and I would urge entrepreneurs and business executives to read them as well. You can find a list of all my favorite business books here: http://www.explosive-growth.com/best-business-books

Book Recommendations: *Little Bets: How Breakthrough Ideas Emerge from Small Discoveries* by Peter Sims and *The Lean Startup: How Today's Entrepreneurs Use Continuous Innovation to Create Radically Successful Businesses* by Eric Ries.

We took some time to lick our wounds from that costly and damaging marketing bust, then restarted the brainstorming about how to grow the user base, because time was of the essence.

We knew how to get a good amount of press coverage, because we had already been on some shows like Geraldo and the Mike and Juliet Show, but getting a lot of signups all at once still eluded us. The goal then became to figure out how to leverage that press coverage to obtain the bigger influx of users that we needed. That was when we discovered the fine art of newsjacking.

NEWSJACKING WITH COLLEGE BASKETBALL AND CELEBRITY CROTCH SHOTS

Take a hot button current event, combine it with some data relevant to your industry, arrive at a hypothesis that may or may not be crazy, and the result is massive publicity. That's the formula for the concept we call newsjacking.

The first time we put this idea to work and realized that we had something very useful was when the Duke University Blue Devils lost in the opening round of the 2007 NCAA Men's Basketball Tournament. Although Duke was far from a powerhouse that year, it was still a shocking defeat, because they had a tradition of deep tournament runs. For them to lose in the opening round was quite the stunner, and more than depressing for the alumni and current student base.

Seizing the opportunity to steal publicity, we piggybacked off this story and created controversy through our own press release that drove attention to our website. The press release stated that the shocking tournament loss made

Duke students so upset and depressed that they flocked to online dating sites to cure their depression (misery loves company), and we provided some data to back it up.

About a week later, we got an email from the school newspaper, the *Duke Chronicle*, asking for some more data around the Duke's students' online dating activity. They ran a follow-up story on it, and it quickly became a hot-button issue on campus. The story ended up getting republished all over the country, and the *Chronicle* ran another story on it a week later. They interviewed a student who claimed she was in a statistics class, understood all about confounding factors, but found absolutely no correlation between the basketball team losing and online dating, which I thought was hilarious.

The story had gone so viral that I started thinking about how I could take it even further. I wanted to keep the positive momentum going, so I tried to speak to Duke's Hall of Fame basketball coach (Coach K) to ask him if he noticed any depression among the players. Unfortunately, (but not surprisingly) I never got a call back from him. Nonetheless, the insane popularity of the topic made it very clear that we were on to something.

A couple of months later, we seized another opportunity for newsjacking: this time related to Britney Spears, right around the same time she broke up with K-Fed. All the entertainment sites were talking about an awards show scene where she was spotted coming out of her limo, and it was crystal clear to everyone that she wasn't wearing any underwear.

At the time, we'd been thinking about hiring a celebrity to become the face of IAmFreeTonight.com, so the timing was perfect. Our press release stated that we were offering Britney $500 to be our spokesperson, but we had a reputation to uphold and refused to relinquish any of our high moral standards. Therefore, should she accept the offer, and have any other flashing incidents or momentary lapses of character, we would have no choice but to void the offer.

We pitched that to several news outlets, and TMZ absolutely loved it. In fact, they loved it so much that they interviewed me for an article about it where they said, "Lerner has decided that Britney wouldn't be making any public appearances on behalf of his site. He says she's too much of a loose cannon."

MR. AND MS. WRONG USER

Duke's ineptitude in the 2007 NCAA Tournament and Britney's unfortunate camera angle did exactly what we wanted in the short term. We got a lot of initial signups from our newsjacking efforts with those press releases. However, a couple of days after the buzz wore off, the site's activity went right back down to a normal level. We were still lacking the key ingredient for a long-term solution. The users from those marketing efforts simply weren't sticking around, and the only feedback we got was from their signup process, when the user would input something like the following as reasons for joining the site:

- "Read about it on TMZ."
- "Saw something about it on a television show."
- "Heard about it in the news and wanted to give it a try."

Those statements told us that the user had a very low likelihood of sticking around, but they still didn't tell us how to get the right users who would stick around. It was a wake-up call for me, because I needed to do something, and fast. The money was running out, and we needed not just a few thousand signups from a couple of well-timed, well-presented press releases. We needed hundreds of thousands of new users to sign up (and stay) in order to stay afloat.

Self-doubt reared its ugly head. I always thought that if I built a good site with a unique feature that addressed a real pain point for the user, people would come to it. It turns out I was right about that, but I overlooked a potentially devastating problem: we couldn't get a large enough influx of users to stay in business. That's when I started looking for something called the Purple Cow. Unfortunately, I didn't find it—not right away.

#ExplosiveGrowthTip 7: A few fanatical customer advocates are worth more than hundreds or even thousands of casual signups. Fanatical users will supply word-of-mouth growth, while providing the necessary feedback to iterate on the product. Do you have at least twenty fanatical users or a plan to get them?

Book Recommendation: *PyroMarketing: The Four-Step Strategy to Ignite Customer Evangelists and Keep Them for Life* by Greg Stielstra.

IS THAT A PURPLE COW?

Seth Godin, a marketing genius wrote a book called *Purple Cow: Transform Your Business by Being Remarkable.* In that definitive work, he describes the concept of a Purple Cow in the following way:

> "When my family and I were driving through France a few years ago, we were enchanted by the hundreds of storybook cows grazing on picturesque pastures

right next to the highway. For dozens of kilometers, we all gazed out the window, marveling how beautiful everything was.

"Then within twenty minutes, we started ignoring the cows. The new cows were just like the old cows, and what once was amazing was now common. Worse than common. It was boring.

"Cows, after you've seen them for a while, are boring. They may be perfect cows, attractive cows, cows with great personalities, cows lit by beautiful light, but they're still boring.

"A Purple Cow, though. Now *that* would be interesting."

"The essence of the Purple Cow is that it must be remarkable."

The moral of the story is that a product needs to be a Purple Cow—something different, exciting, and remarkable (something worthy of remark). The offering needs to be so unique and exceptional that nothing compares to it, and people want to talk about it.

Book Recommendation: *Purple Cow: Transform Your Business by Being Remarkable*, by Seth Godin.

I thought I had a great concept with IAmFreeTonight. com, but clearly, it wasn't unique enough to be a Purple Cow—maybe some shades of light blue, but definitely not purple. Nobody was stopping the car to get out and say, "Holy crap—it's an online dating site where I can get a date in a few minutes instead of a few days!"

At this point, we had some things that were working well, like a unique product and a knack for getting press. We also had some things that weren't working well. For instance, although our product was unique, it wasn't a Purple Cow, and although we could get press anytime we wanted it, the users we got from those efforts weren't the right users.

I understood what was working for us and what wasn't, and it was only a matter of time before I figured out the breakthrough that would give us an influx of hundreds of thousands of users. I decided we needed to survive long enough to make that magic moment happen. We had to play to our strengths, so we could live to fight another day. That meant outworking other companies in the industry, continuing to innovate, and maintaining awareness of the marketplace. Instinctively, we went into survival mode, trimmed costs to the bare bones, and sure enough, our game-changer presented itself.

The game-changer had been created in the hallowed

halls of Harvard University and was being released to a wider and more public audience. A cocky, but inventive and brilliant dropout named Mark Zuckerberg was about to add a whole new dimension to the way we socialized online. It didn't take me long to appreciate his ingenuity and the potentially disruptive impact his website would have on the online dating industry. We had to seize the opportunity to be part of it. Is that a Purple Cow I see on its way over here?

3

DOES OUR PRODUCT SUCK?

"You can market your ass off, but if your product sucks, you're dead."

—GARY VAYNERCHUK, AMERICAN SERIAL ENTREPRENEUR AND FOUR-TIME BEST-SELLING AUTHOR

In the spring of 2007, IMFT was acquiring a few thousand new users every month organically, which was decent, but even if they were all the right users, it still wasn't enough. We needed a much bigger influx of users, because the initial financial runway we built—even after I doubled my estimate—was running out. Something was wrong somewhere, but I wasn't sure what it was yet.

Suddenly, a much more frightening possibility crept into my mind. I began to wonder if maybe our product just sucked. It was more likely an evil form of paranoia from my subconscious mind than a legitimate fear, because I always believed we had a unique idea and a great product. It's only natural for some self-doubt to creep in, however, when the clock is ticking on your business.

COULD THIS BE MAGIC?

These days, there are a lot of early indicators to tell if a product sucks, or at least whether it's remarkable or not:

- Are people tweeting about it?
- Are people sharing it on Facebook?
- What is the overall social media buzz?

But ten years ago, when SNAP Interactive (the parent company of our dating apps) was starting to grow, the landscape was much different.

Twitter only began in 2006, so tweeting was still reserved mostly for bird calls.

Facebook had barely begun to expand beyond the college walls, so that wasn't a factor either.

Analytics platforms hadn't developed to the levels we find today, so it wasn't as easy to track and analyze every piece of user activity and engagement metric in real time.

Therefore, it was a little harder for me to determine if our product sucked, despite having a decent number of users. Ultimately, what I learned was that if something isn't jumping out as extraordinary right away, there might be a problem. Something magical should be very clear from the outset.

While still wondering if our product sucked or not, I asked some family and friends their opinions. They told me all sorts of wonderful things to offer their encouragement, support, and probably feed my ego at the same time, but they didn't shed any light on why our product wasn't flourishing.

"Your product's great, Cliff!"

"I love IMFT—it's way better than Match!"

"Everybody should be using your online dating app."

All these glowing responses only fueled my concern even more because, if all these people really thought my site was so amazing, why hadn't they told their friends about it, and why weren't they using it more often?

#ExplosiveGrowthTip 8: Having a remarkable product is not subjective. Either people remark and it grows organically or they don't. Are people remarking about your product?

A bunch of different anecdotal notions crept into my head at that point. We had a unique product, but just because something is unique, doesn't mean it's a Purple Cow. The timing might not have been right, like our situation with the wingman concept. The user experience might have been too clunky. Or, the idea might just not have added enough value for the user to switch to it.

I knew something was inherently wrong with the product, and it had something to do with a metric key to the success of any business: retention. We were getting great press, but it didn't amount to enough new users. Perhaps most importantly, the new users that we were getting weren't the right ones, because they weren't using the site after their initial signup. It became obvious that the current path wasn't going to get us where we needed to be.

We had some good things working in our favor: the product was unique enough and we were getting a limited but steady flow of new users. I still believed greatly in our product and our company, but I needed to make some magic happen.

THE 10X EFFECT

We needed a product that was doing something not just slightly better, but massively better—ten times better— than the other dating sites on the market. That's called the 10X effect, and we clearly didn't have that with IMFT. The biggest reason we needed something that was 10x better was because of what's referred to as switching costs for the user. On dating and social networking sites such as Facebook, users have already invested substantial time in uploading photos, posting content, adding their friends, etc. Therefore, even if a marginally better product comes along, it's not worth a user's time to start over. The new product needs to be ten times better than the competition for the user to justify investing their time in it.

ALL PAWS: THE 10X EFFECT
IN PET ADOPTION

My brother, Darrell, who was a cofounder of the company and an absolutely crucial factor in its success, is also a serial entrepreneur with some heavy-duty legal and accounting experience. His role within Snap Interactive, however, was becoming increasingly undefined as the company grew, and he continued hiring his replacements in key business functions that he once managed individually. Sure enough, in 2013, inspiration called upon him, and he answered by founding a pet adoption platform called AllPaws.

Darrell has always been a pet lover, so he recognized an unmet need for people looking to adopt pets. His idea was built upon the lessons he learned from his experience in the online dating world with the 10X effect, and how to apply some similar functionality to build a user experience that was ten times better in a different industry.

The 10X effect taught him that he didn't need to recreate the wheel. He just needed to understand his users' pain points, address them, and make the user experience ten times better than what the rest of the industry was offering.

When people start their search to adopt a pet, they usually have very specific search criteria. For instance, they may want a hypoallergenic breed with a gentle disposition, who is trainable and good with children. Or, for some reason, they might want a rabid Rottweiler who eats steroids like kibble and has a taste for human flesh. Either way, Darrell realized people didn't currently have the ability to perform a detailed search for pets using variables like health, behavior, and compatibility. All totaled, there were at least thirty search filters for users to select from. So, he created a website and app that allowed people to do that.

AllPaws isn't all that different from a good online dating site. The shelters have the ability to create a very detailed profile for their adoptable pets, and prospective new pet parents can search for specific criteria to establish a match. Darrell simply used the lessons he learned as a cofounder of Snap Interactive to make the pet adoption experience ten times better. He sold the company a few years later to a multi-billion-dollar company, PetSmart, and the site still exists today. If you're a pet lover and looking to adopt a new fur baby, I recommend checking it out.

#ExplosiveGrowthTip 9: A marginally better product is worthless. It needs to be at least ten times better. Have you quantified how much better your product's core offering is than the competition?

#ExplosiveGrowthTip 10: You can often find success at the intersection of passion and expertise. Are you passionate about the problem your product solves?

#ExplosiveGrowthTip 11: Have you looked outside your

industry for new solutions and approaches to solve the problem in order to create the 10X experience?

Book Recommendation: *Zero to One: Notes on Startups, or How to Build the Future*, by Peter Thiel.

The biggest pain point with IMFT was the amount of time it took to build a user profile, which included finding and uploading several profile photos. The whole process took several minutes, and in the modern fast-paced, on-demand world, that was far too long for most users.

What if there was a way for users to upload a complete profile with their best pictures and all the necessary information with just one click? That would have been an online dating site that was ten, no, make that at least a hundred times better than anything else out there. If only there was a way for us to do that.

4

BET THE COMPANY

"You miss 100 percent of the shots you don't take."

—WAYNE GRETZKY, "THE GREAT ONE"

One fateful night in early May of 2007, I once again had another epiphany that proved crucial to the longevity of my business. This time it came from an article I read about an emerging website called, Facebook, which wasn't nearly the colossal online presence that it is today. In fact, Facebook had only just recently opened its virtual doors to non-college students. In its infancy, Facebook was exclusively available to Zuck's Harvard brethren. Then, it opened to a few more colleges, before it finally became available to the general public.

The article described how Facebook was building a platform and an API that enabled companies to build apps for their products within the website. More importantly, by building apps for this platform, those companies would gain access to the friend list and profile information of any user who signed up, while enabling users to 'invite' their friends to use these applications and access other areas of the user's profile, such as publishing to their "wall."

PURPLE COW APPROACHING

There was something about the ability to reach a different network of friends, or one's "social graph" as Facebook calls it, every time one user signed up, and that was very interesting to me. Previous research taught me that most people met their significant other through friends, and that's still true today. I asked myself, "What if I could find a way to leverage Facebook's social graph for IAmFreeTonight.com?"

The idea of a platform API was a foreign concept at the time, so it seemed a bit risky to invest very heavily into something so unproven. But I had to take chances at this point—in basketball terms, we needed a buzzer beater. My team had put up a good fight throughout the game, but we were down by two points, time was running out, and

I had the ball in my hands behind the three-point arc. I had to take my best shot.

I called our lead programmer, Mike Sherov the next day, and I said to him, "Mike, I just read an article about something called Facebook. I want to build an app for it—a Facebook app."

He responded very appropriately, asking me, "What's a Facebook app?"

"I have no idea yet," I said, "but I have a really strong feeling that we should build one anyway."

Mike sensed my fervor and acquiesced accordingly, "Okay, so, what do you want me to do?"

With my intensity building, I said, "Drop everything you're doing and build a Facebook app. Figure it out."

Over the next week or so, Mike spent all his time doing some intense research about the new Facebook platform while trying to figure out how to build an app for it. He came back to me and said, "Okay, I think we can basically put our website within Facebook. Is that what you want to do?"

I replied, "That's exactly what I want to do. I'm not sure what we'll do with it yet, but I'll figure that part out. Great job!"

IF YOU BUILD IT, THEY WILL COME

No, the cyber-geek version of Moonlight Graham from *Field of Dreams* wasn't happening; I wasn't getting subliminal whispers in my office headset about how to get a massive influx of the right users to IMFT. But, some voice in my head must have instinctively known that building an app for Facebook was the right decision for our company, because something made me go all in with it, and sure enough, the users did come.

On May 14, 2007 Facebook officially launched their platform to the general public, and they did so with several launch partners that I had never heard of before. Some of them were actually nothing more than single developers, but they were all getting thousands of new users each day by piggybacking off of Facebook's new 'Application Platform.' That kind of organic growth was unheard of for a dating site, so I figured if some of those launch partners could do it, so could we. At the time, there was still only a handful of apps on the site, and I knew it was only a matter of time before some of the big boys figured it out. Therefore, despite knowing next to nothing about what we were getting into, I was more convinced than ever that we needed to be an early adopter of this technology and go all-in with Facebook.

OPEN ACCESS TO FACEBOOK: CRAZY OR GENIUS?

At the time, the prevailing opinion was that Mark Zuckerberg was crazy to launch such an open platform to any developer. By all accounts, Facebook was doing just fine on its own, so why give away access to their millions of users and data to any random company? Nobody had ever done anything similar on that scale before, and the thought was that companies would take advantage and simply try to port all the users to their own websites while ruining the Facebook experience for their own gain.

Zuckerberg saw it differently, as he knew that a site like Facebook would need to constantly innovate to stay relevant. He took a gamble and believed that the world's top companies and developers would soon be flocking to Facebook to build applications on it (remember, that's where the eyeballs were). It effectively served as unlimited innovation for the site, which would keep users coming back for the long run. Ultimately, building a Facebook app became a top priority for nearly every tech company, and the launch of the Facebook platform began a new era of super-growth that was key to its ultimate success.

The first iteration of our Facebook app was exactly as Mike said it would be; the app simply consisted of the registration page for IMFT within Facebook, which would then drive users out of Facebook, and onto our website. This first version of our Facebook app instantly netted a couple thousand users all on its own. Also, there was only a limited number of apps available for download on Facebook in those early days, so users would usually just go to the app directory and install the entire set, which probably helped our numbers quite a bit.

I CAN SEE CLEARLY NOW?

That first iteration of our Facebook app gave us more users in its first day than we had gotten in any previous day of doing business. At the same time, I saw several other no-name companies getting five to ten thousand users daily, all organically. I once again thought to myself, "If they can do it, we can do it. It's just a matter of who's the hungriest and smartest." I knew we could win that battle, because we had great talent on our side and even more drive. At that point, failure was not an option. There was simply too much for me to lose, because going back to Wall Street and battling the club-goers at 5:00 a.m. for a taxi was not an appealing option.

Another thing I saw very early on was how quickly Facebook was growing. I had the pleasure of meeting a lot of the people who helped create the platform at a conference I attended, which was also one of the first times anybody heard Mark Zuckerberg speak publicly.

These people were some of the smartest people I had ever met. They were constantly thinking five to ten years ahead in time, which is why Facebook is alive and thriving today, while many of their competitors have long since disappeared. The subjects and depth of discussions they were having were on another level, which made me more confident than ever in their future. By contrast, MySpace, the largest social network in the world at the time (who would soon launch their own platform), was calling me to convince me to buy more ads for my application, while their website was crashing and barely functional.

Meanwhile, Facebook was discussing their crystal-clear vision of how they would one day have the most intelligent ad network in the world. They kept mentioning this new type of employee called a data scientist. These insanely smart computer science nerd types would analyze all the data, and use it to accurately predict things like when and where their users' next vacation would be, what they will want to eat next, and even when they will get in or out of a relationship (which could be determined based on photo viewing habits of certain "friends"). That unbelievably in-depth use of data absolutely blew my mind. They were laying the groundwork for what years later would become the world's most successful ad network.

The user experience (UX) was something that was also of the utmost importance to them. They recognized that the UX on other social networks like Friendster and MySpace had become quite poor, as there was more of an emphasis on short-term revenues and profitability. The interfaces on those sites were often very slow and completely cluttered with spam, advertisements, and other load-time slowing graphics.

With their competition foolishly focused on short-term profits, Facebook was making a crucial discovery. Facebook realized that if a user got seven or more friends in their first ten days, the user became "addicted" to Facebook and came back over and over. This is called the "aha" moment, when a user understands a product's value to them. To ensure that new users reached that magic number of seven friends, Facebook dedicated some of their best engineers to figuring out how to surface that long-lost cousin or friend from first grade, and imported them into their users' suggested friends list. It grew their network effect substantially, and it proved to be a brilliant strategy that paid obvious, long-term dividends and gave them the sustained success all start-ups strive to achieve.

The people at Facebook were very young, aware, and had such a long-term view of what would drive their sustained success (a superior user experience) from the outset, that it was obvious to any developer that with these people at the helm, Facebook was going to be as big as anything we had ever seen. From my early impression at the conference and our resounding early success as a Facebook app, it was clear to me that we needed to piggyback on Facebook's success as much as possible. Fortunately, we were in on the ground floor.

 #ExplosiveGrowthTip 12: Do you know what your product's "aha" moment is? If not, figure it out, and focus on optimizing that experience for all users.

WHY FACEBOOK?

Contrary to what many people may think, Facebook was not the world's first social network. It wasn't MySpace or Friendster either, both of which had some moderate success before Facebook's groundbreaking arrival. The world's first social network was a site called sixdegrees, which was founded by a personal mentor and very close friend of mine, named Andrew Weinreich.

Sixdegrees actually hit the cyber landscape more than ten years before Zuckerberg's game-changer, way back in 1997. Andrew is one of the most brilliant entrepreneurial minds I've ever known, but sixdegrees is no longer around, and Facebook dominates social networking. What happened? What is so special about Facebook that has made it one of the most valuable companies in the world?

One of the greatest lessons Andrew taught me is that timing is indeed everything. It's important to not confuse this notion with being first, because having the best timing doesn't necessarily mean being first. In some instances, being first can actually work against you.

In Andrew's case, sixdegrees was first to arrive in the social media marketplace, long before Facebook, but it lacked one feature that has come to completely characterize Facebook: pictures.

Note: Sensing he was onto something big, Andrew authored what's known as the "Six-Degree Patent," which explains how people are connected online. The patent has since become very prominent, and is now owned by LinkedIn.

Sixdegrees was ahead of its time in a lot of ways, but one very significant factor was that the supporting technology—particularly digital cameras—weren't in widespread use at the time. Andrew knew that photos would be a big factor in the success of social networking, but there was no clear path to getting them incorporated into the site. At one point, he evaluated having users snail mail their photos, and then hiring an assembly line of people to scan and upload them into users' profiles. Although this was a clever workaround, Andrew ultimately determined it wasn't practical.

"Tagging" someone didn't exist yet either. That was another crucial nuance to the positive influence of photos that propelled those later social networking sites.

The crazy thing about timing a market is that it's almost impossible to predict when seismic change will occur. Andrew sold sixdegrees in 1999, when very few people had digital pictures of themselves. By 2003, there were more phones with digital cameras than there were standalone digital cameras. A new wave of social networking was born, beginning with Friendster, then MySpace and finally, Facebook.

The reported sale price of sixdegrees was $125 million, so it still paid off, but not in quite the same way as Facebook. Some experts are predicting Facebook could someday become the first company to be valued at $1 trillion. Ironically, several of these experts are my former

Wall Street colleagues and analysts, who laughed at me in 2007 when I said Facebook would be worth $100 billion in a few years, and whom I urged to learn about it as soon as they could.

In the end, was Facebook vastly superior to anything else in the industry? Not really, because the features and basic concept weren't very different from sixdegrees or even Friendster and MySpace, but the timing and long-term vision were right. Supporting technologies, including the rapid adoption of mobile phones and the ease of uploading photos online, had come around, and the user was finally ready to adopt it.

BE THE SMARTEST IN THE WORLD AT SOMETHING

I met my friend and mentor, Andrew, one January at a conference for online dating executives called iDate. At the time, Andrew was running what was arguably the first mobile dating site called MeetMoi (Andrew was the first to do a lot of things). One of the most impactful things Andrew taught me at that conference was, "I've learned that you've got to be the smartest in the world at something to win. Cliff, I think you're the smartest in the world at viral marketing on Facebook."

It sounded like a pompous term to claim myself as "the smartest in the world" at something, but it was very important to recognize my strengths as a leader. However, Andrew doesn't say anything that he doesn't mean, so those words provided me with the courage I needed to triple down on Facebook virality. I placed all my efforts on understanding the Facebook platform as best I could. Andrew's words gave me the confidence I needed to shut down the site that wasn't going to get me there (IMFT), and go all in on a new site that would.

Deciding to ultimately shut down IMFT was not only a huge deal, but it was also a shock to employees, investors, and any stakeholders who were there to see it happen. I was choosing an unproven product that was only a few weeks old, over an established product that was two full years in the making and had a user base in the tens of thousands.

But my logic was, I wanted to look forward, not backward, and stop throwing good money at a product with limited potential. IMFT had lots of distractions, and it would require time and money just to deal with the inevitable bugs and server issues—crucial minutes and dollars that we couldn't afford to spare. In the end, this decision was the equivalent of removing a thousand-pound gorilla from our corporate backs, and it had an immediately favorable impact on the growth of our new Facebook application.

 #ExplosiveGrowthTip 13: Are there projects you're keeping alive by ignoring the sunk-cost principle (or for emotional and non-practical reasons)? If so, shut them down now to free up more valuable time and focus.

From this realization, IMFT evolved into MeetNewPeople (MNP), which was a dating app with a simple user interface. When the user logged in, they saw a picture of another user with a question: *Do you like this person, yes or no?*

One key result we learned was that driving people off of Facebook to IMFT wasn't effective. Besides the fact that users simply didn't want to leave Facebook, we learned it was much more beneficial to get users to take as many actions as possible within Facebook, so we could publish to their News Feed as often as possible and access their network of friends. Learning how important retention was to creating a sustainable and growing product, we relented and stopped trying to drive users off of Facebook to access IMFT, which paid off immediately.

"I've not failed. I've just found 10,000 different ways that won't work."

—THOMAS EDISON, AMERICA'S GREATEST INVENTOR

MNP served as an interim app to use as a testing ground for any idea we could conceive of. It was a bridge to get us to Are You Interested? (AYI), which we officially launched on August 14, 2007. Our goal with this interim website was to test as many features and ideas as possible to see what produced the most growth and highest retention, while learning about how to best leverage the Facebook platform and its unique features to grow virally.

YOU CAN'T IMPROVE WHAT YOU DON'T MEASURE

We quickly realized the key to our success wasn't about coming up with the next brilliant idea, but how quickly we could run tests on our users. This meant building robust analytics. The more tests we ran, the more we learned, and the more we succeeded. The tests we ran ranged in complexity from in-depth new features to simple changes such as testing different background colors. Testing different background colors showed us how simple changes had massive impacts on user behavior. In case anyone is wondering, yes, a pink background for females did lead to substantially more activity from that demographic.

Constant experimentation and robust real-time analytics became core to our corporate culture where we would embrace failure, because it meant we were learning more about our users. After visiting Facebook's offices, we learned they had a similar culture, and their developers' mantra was, "Move fast and break things."

#ExplosiveGrowthTip 14: Perfect is the enemy of shipped. Creating the perfect feature indicates making lots of assumptions without gathering user feedback and data, and will take significantly more time. Are you continuing to work on features that are polished enough to put in front of a few customers now and get feedback?

#ExplosiveGrowthTip 15: Building product and testing features without robust analytics is like driving blindfolded—it won't end well. Do you have an effective dashboard with all your key metrics?

Book Recommendations: *You Should Test That: Conversion Optimization for More Leads, Sales and Profit or The Art and Science of Optimized Marketing,* by Chris Goward, and *Sprint: How to Solve Big Problems and Test New Ideas in Just Five Days* by Jake Knapp.

Thanks to the rigorous testing, thorough data analysis, and site optimizations we previously performed on MNP, AYI acquired around 10,000 new users per day upon launch, all without spending a dime on user acquisition. At that point, we all knew we were sitting on a goldmine!

5

THE GROWTH ROCKET (100,000 NEW USERS IN ONE DAY!)

"Virality isn't luck. It's not magic. And it's not random. There's a science behind why people talk and share. A recipe. A formula, even."

—JONAH BERGER, BEST-SELLING
AUTHOR OF *CONTAGIOUS*

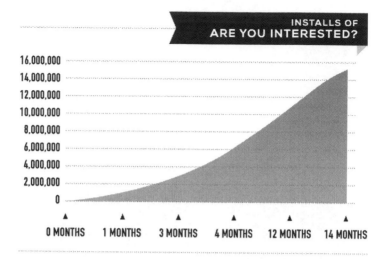

INSTALLS OF ARE YOU INTERESTED?

0 MONTHS	1 MONTHS	3 MONTHS	4 MONTHS	12 MONTHS	14 MONTHS

16,000,000
14,000,000
12,000,000
10,000,000
8,000,000
6,000,000
4,000,000
2,000,000
0

Taking our product from the rudimentary MNP to the much more polished AYI involved grueling eighteen-hour days of constant testing and optimizing, with the goals of getting users to invite more friends, and spending more time browsing other users on the app. We had to figure out what worked best and what didn't to get to the result we desired, which was becoming experts in going viral on Facebook.

We also knew we couldn't accept a sub-par feature implementation, because it was only a matter of time before the big boys discovered the Facebook virality gold mine we were sitting on. The big boys had unlimited resources at their disposal that we couldn't possibly match. Therefore, we needed to build a huge lead and constantly push ourselves to the limits. For example, we knew that showing profiles continuously with no lag time in between (similar to what Tinder does now) would make the experience amazing. It wasn't an easy goal to accomplish at the time—it took weeks of hard work with numerous iterations and a refusal to accept mediocrity.

Whereas perfect was a misuse of resources for most features, exceptions to the rule did exist. There were certain critical user experience items that we needed to be as near to perfect as possible.

GOING VIRAL

Brian Balfour is recognized as a growth expert. He has started and grown multiple VC-backed companies with millions of users and is the former VP of Growth at HubSpot. Brian runs a terrific blog discussing the latest growth strategies and techniques (http://www.coelevate.com) and leads masterclasses on the topic at http://www.reforge.com. Some thoughts from Brian on virality are as follows:

> "Going viral" has been the holy grail for Silicon Valley since the mid-90s, but the concepts behind virality have been around for about a hundred years or more. It's understood that the first chain letters appeared in the early 1900s. As the internet emerged and plat-

forms such as email, Facebook, and mobile devices connected everyone, fuel was poured onto the viral fire.

"In its simplest form, virality is about how one user or customer helps to get another user or customer. Think about it as a loop: a user signs up, they take some action, that action leads to another user signing up, and the loop starts over.

"There are different flavors of these viral loops, such as the following examples:

- **Organic Invites**—A Dropbox user shares a folder with their colleague. That colleague signs up for Dropbox as a result.
- **Casual Contact**—A Hotmail user sends an email with the signature "P.S., I love you. Get your free email at Hotmail." The recipient sees that and also signs up for Hotmail.
- **Incentivized Referrals**—An Uber user invites a friend to receive $10 in credit. That friend joins Uber as a result.

"Not all viral loops are created equally. Some are more effective than others. The effectiveness of the viral loop is measured by its K-factor. The K-factor measures how many additional users the original user will bring in when they sign up for the product. For example, if someone says their K-factor is 0.5, that means one new user will be brought in for every two new users acquired. The Holy Grail is achieved anytime a K-factor is greater than one."

INCENTIVIZING THE USER

Incentivizing the user to invite their friends had a massive effect where we got over 100,000 new users in one day, and it proved to be the key to going viral on Facebook. The key was figuring out the right incentives to drive the user to take action. There are many nuances to making incentives successful, but it all comes down to giving users a compelling reason to invite their friends and an equally compelling reason for the friends to accept the invite and try out the product.

On a dating app, users (especially men) are generally looking to get more incoming messages. So, giving users an opportunity to get more attention (thus more possible messages) became the basis of our reward system.

#ExplosiveGrowthTip 16: Can you identify the one thing about your product that users want more of? Have you tested offering this to them for free if they get some friends to join?

To provide the necessary reward system, we challenged our users to invite five new friends, and as a reward for their efforts, they would appear higher in search results, which would lead to more matches and messages. Eureka! Almost every user invited five of their friends.

After that, we thought that a good idea would be to up the ante, so we increased the challenge to ten friends, and almost every user accepted that challenge as well.

The maximum number of friends that Facebook allowed us to ask for was twenty, and that number gave us thousands of new users every day on the app. We also realized that small changes in language could have drastic effects on the results. The following is an example of how we changed the language ever so slightly to tap into a user's emotions, and get them to act:

- Iteration one: Invite your friends!
- Iteration two: Invite five friends for higher placement in search results!
- Iteration three: Invite twenty friends for higher placement in search results!
- Iteration four: Invite five friends for more matches!
- Iteration five: Invite twenty friends for more matches!
- Iteration six: Invite five friends to find out which of your friends likes you!
- Iteration seven: Invite twenty friends to find out which of your friends likes you!

By changing a few words around, we got drastically better results. We learned that language is a big part of effective communication with the user, and even subtle changes to the copy had a big impact on user behavior, and the ultimate success of our business.

One key item we learned in this process was that "selling the benefit" was far more effective than selling the feature. The feature is what something is, and the benefit is how it improves lives. For example, people weren't enamored enough with the "feature" of getting higher placement in search results, because it wasn't clear to them why this was important. But getting more matches, or finding out which of their friends liked them was an emotional benefit they could associate with some value. Those small changes were a big part of how we got to over a hundred thousand new users per day.

Most products are missing a big opportunity if their copy focuses on selling the feature, instead of its benefit. Marketing efforts should concentrate on answering the consumer's question, "What's in it for me?"

 #ExplosiveGrowthTip 17: When writing copy, sell the benefit, not the feature. Are you selling the benefit?

A THOUSAND SONGS IN YOUR POCKET VS. A FIVE-GIGABYTE HARD DRIVE

A great example of selling the benefit and not the feature is when Steve Jobs introduced the original iPod. The feature was a five-gigabyte hard drive, but the benefit (and the slogan they used) was "one thousand songs in your pocket."

CONSTANT TESTING IS CRITICAL

We saw the slightest change in copy (including something as innocuous as a color change) had a 20 percent or more improvement on the results. Believing that our success hinged upon our ability to learn quicker than our competitors, we built an internal testing platform that enabled us to run over one thousand simultaneous experiments.

Rigorous testing is something that any business—even something as simple as a corner store—could benefit from. Test what the sign in the window says. Test product placement. Test what's in the display case. Test pricing. Even a bunch of small increases taken together might equal a large increase.

Constant testing and experimentation is critical for every business to embrace as part of their culture and can be implemented regardless of the industry. Several small wins can lead to massive results as each win compounds with the next. For example, not only were we able to improve the copy on the *friend inviter* to increase the number of invites, but we also optimized the subject and copy in the email invite that the friends received. There are many touchpoints in a product's funnel, from the initial user experience until payment (signup flow, email subject, email content and frequency, payment pages, etc.), and the ultimate conversion is only as good as the weakest link.

 #ExplosiveGrowthTip 18: If you're not running tests, start now. Do you plan to run at least three tests in the next thirty days?

WHERE ARE THE EYEBALLS?

The old saying goes, "The three most important factors of having a successful business are location, location, and location." Location, location, location may still apply to brick-and-mortar stores like restaurants and retail shops, but I think that old saying needs an update to account for today's virtual marketplace. The three most important factors for a successful online dating site (or any online business) to rapidly acquire users are platforms, platforms, and platforms.

What I soon learned was that a unique product was great, but knowing how to leverage a highly visible marketing channel (like Facebook) to get it in front of many users was even more crucial. We needed that marketing channel to make our unique product thrive. Growing slowly would scare off investors, drain cash resources, and not provide invaluable user feedback, so growing quickly through a highly effective marketing channel is crucial for most start-ups. That's when the importance of marketing for an online business really hit me.

 #ExplosiveGrowthTip 19: Many of today's billion-dollar companies succeeded by growing on top of other platforms. Are you testing integrations with emerging and established platforms?

I DON'T CARE HOW GREAT YOUR PRODUCT IS. TELL ME HOW YOU'RE GOING TO GROW...FAST

People approach me all the time for advice on investments and ideas. The first thing I ask them is, "What's your plan to acquire thousands of targeted users?" Inevitably, most people's response is, "I don't know exactly, but my product is so friggin' unique, it's going to blow people away! We're going to get a ton of press and everybody will fall in love with us." That's when I give them the history of my company and our product. I tell them that I had a product that I thought was pretty damned unique, and we were outstanding at getting press, but it didn't matter until we found the right platform to access millions in our target audience.

I've learned that entrepreneurs and businesses who have a unique (and cost-effective) plan to market their product to achieve scale have an outstanding chance of success, but a great product without a great growth strategy will likely fail.

A GREAT GROWTH STRATEGY ALWAYS TRUMPS A GREAT PRODUCT

Dating sites (and many other businesses) have similar products that are hard to distinguish from each other. Yet some achieve enormous success while others don't. When one looks back at the thriving and successful online dating companies, the common denominator was that each one had a distinct growth strategy that leveraged the product's unique offering. I'd argue this is true of most other industries as well.

Many of the world's largest online dating sites grew, not because their product was unbelievably good, nor because they had large marketing budgets, but because they executed a brilliant growth strategy—a "growth rocket."

GROWTH ROCKET

Consider a "growth rocket" to be a unique and inexpensive growth tactic that leverages your product's key differentiator to cause a sudden and massive user increase.

Let's look at some of the most successful online dating sites of the past decade (plus Twitter) and examine how they achieved their extraordinary growth.

TINDER

Need some examples of how marketing is the key to making a unique product grow at a high enough rate to survive? First, look at Tinder—a company I'll discuss in detail later on. Tinder's popularity skyrocketed when they threw college launch parties targeting popular fraternities, sororities, and attractive coeds. I can just picture the marketing meeting to plan that event.

"Here's an idea: What if we throw parties at a bunch of different college campuses around the country? We invite the sororities with the hottest college girls we can find, and have the frat guys show up. Then, tell everyone to download our app to get into the party. After that, they can swipe left or right all night. By the next morning, the entire campus will have our app, and they'll be telling everyone about it!"

It worked to perfection. They threw one ripper of a college blowout after another, and the app spread like wildfire. It was what business school types call the perfect product-market fit. Since then, numerous other companies have tried the same strategy, but it never worked as well as what Tinder did. Just because something worked once, doesn't mean it's going to keep working. Successful ideas still need vision, creativity, and brilliant execution behind them.

"You need to identify social influencers in small areas, see who the influencers are, and target them. That's how we spread throughout college campuses and other social scenes."

—WHITNEY WOLFE, FORMER TINDER VP OF
MARKETING AND FOUNDER OF BUMBLE

BUMBLE

Bumble is very similar to Tinder with one key difference, women have to initiate contact first. Although this is a compelling feature, it's hardly something that would lead to a new dating site getting millions of users in just a couple of years.

It's once again the marketing strategy and brilliant foresight that propelled Bumble to become a market leader so soon.

Bumble discovered how powerful online influencers were very early in the game. Frankly, they used a concept similar to the rationale of the campus influencers that Tinder used, except Bumble used an online approach.

Posts touting Bumble appeared all over Instagram accounts, which led to massive visibility and rapid adoption before most people were even familiar with the term, "online influencer." It's also not a surprise that the founder of Bumble, Whitney Wolfe, was also the VP of Marketing at Tinder, and largely credited with Tinder's college marketing strategy.

Another smart thing Bumble initially did was form a strategic partnership with Andrey Andreev, the founder of Badoo, one of the largest social networking sites in the world. This partnership gave Bumble access to the vast resources of a large technology company (including capital and engineering talent) so they could hit the ground running. It would greatly accelerate Bumble's product development and enhance their chances of success as they were able to avoid many of the traditional start-up pain points and pitfalls.

JSWIPE

There were two Jewish-oriented Tinder copycats for a while in the online dating space. In the beginning, JCrush had an early lead for market share over a competitor called JSwipe, which was growing at a good rate as well. However, JSwipe partnered with a huge Jewish organization called Birthright, which gave them a massive influx of potential users and helped them "JCrush" their competition. That singular affiliation with an organization with a massive marketing reach propelled JSwipe to success, and their app is flourishing today because of it. Note: JSwipe was acquired by Spark Networks, the owner of Jdate.com, for $7 million in October 2015.

 #ExplosiveGrowthTip 20: Have you targeted a partnership that would provide massive visibility and growth for you?

PLENTY OF FISH (POF.COM)

Plenty of Fish dove (pardon the pun) into search engine optimization (SEO) tactics to get in front of a massive number of users. Their founder, Markus Frind, is a brilliant entrepreneur. He is the pioneer of long tail SEO for online dating sites. Long tail SEO refers to niche search terms, usually with three or more words, such as "free online dating in Nevada" or "man seeking woman in Las Vegas." In their aggregate, those terms end up being much more valuable than the broader search terms such as "singles," or "online dating." Frind perfected a system for his site to get ranked for almost any term applicable to online dating long before most people had even heard of the term SEO. Plenty of Fish ultimately became one of the largest dating sites in the world and sold for $580 million to IAC in 2016.

AREYOUINTERESTED? AND ZOOSK

AYI and Zoosk are known to be the two most successful Facebook dating apps, each achieving over a hundred million users. Both were able to grow rapidly by building their dating app on top of the Facebook platform very early, and they built a feature set that leveraged the viral opportunities to grow within Facebook. Without the monster platform of Facebook, these products likely would have never existed. These opportunities are as abundant as ever and start-ups should spend substantial time analyzing and testing opportunities to leverage large platforms for growth.

TWITTER

The concept of a unique growth strategy being much more valuable than a great product isn't limited to online dating. Great growth strategies are crucial in any industry; consider Twitter's growth rocket.

Believe it or not, Twitter was not designed to be used as a method for the President of the United States to get his or her opinion—right or wrong—out to the American people at three o'clock in the morning. Twitter was made to be a method of concise communication (tweets) from one to many (although you could communicate one to one also). It's a very unique, quick, and efficient way to broadcast news and information, but it didn't start out as a ball of fire. Just like some of the online dating sites we mentioned, Twitter also needed to find a way to grow exponentially.

Going viral for Twitter happened when they put their technology on display for all the early tech adopters at the South by Southwest (SXSW) conference. Twitter put televisions all over the conference floor showing a real-time stream of tweets with the #SXSW hashtag, and encouraged people to use Twitter to broadcast their messages, like where the hottest party was, which talks were best, and so on. Everyone at the conference became glued to the #SXSW stream on the televisions scattered around the conference. From one marketing success at the SXSX tech conference, Twitter invented the hashtag and became an instant sensation.

In each case above, it was the unique marketing channel or growth rocket strategy that enabled these products to achieve their massive growth, and not because they had an incredible product or a large marketing budget. As a matter of fact, none of those strategies required a large marketing budget, if any budget at all. However, each product did find a growth strategy that complemented the uniqueness of the product, enabling them to get exposure to thousands (if not millions) of targeted users for free.

#ExplosiveGrowthTip 21: Your growth strategy can't be an afterthought. A great product with a poor or traditional marketing plan will have poor results. Do you have a growth rocket strategy?

THEY HATE YOU BECAUSE THEY CARE

One of the very first signs that we were on to something much bigger and better with MNP, (which ultimately became AYI), was that people started to really care about the product. From the first day MNP launched, we got hundreds (and some days, thousands) of posts to the app's message board.

One of the most popular threads in the early days of MNP was an accusation that the product and company were anti-gay, which was categorically untrue. The incorrect accusation arose from the lack of search functionality for gay men or women on our app. In reality, it was a stupid oversight on my part, not an intentional omission. We were definitely *not* anti-gay, but nonetheless, the thread was picking up a lot of momentum.

What people didn't know was that we still had only one developer (Mike) for an app that had a ton of traffic. The site was growing by leaps and bounds, and there was simply no possibility of taking Mike away from his plethora of duties—mostly focused on keeping the app stable and online—to develop search functionality of that magnitude. Unfortunately, that explanation wasn't good enough to quell the outspoken and angry users voicing their displeasure.

Despite the unpleasantness of that experience, I learned a big lesson concerning the absolute value of users' emotions. People getting really angry and actively voicing their concerns about my product meant they cared about it. Conversely, if nobody was saying anything, that would have indicated a problem, because it would have meant nobody cared enough to call me out for it.

#ExplosiveGrowthTip 22: If people are complaining about something, it means the product is good enough that they care about it. The real problem is when no one's complaining. Is anybody complaining about your product?

THIS COULD BE MAGIC

Just because people showed me they cared by hating me didn't mean we were necessarily onto something magical, however. Hatred indicates a lot of things, but on its own, it's not enough to constitute magic.

Does hatred show passion? Yes.

Does that sort of response show they care? Yes.

Does taking the time to express their distaste for something about your product show that it is worthy of their time and attention? Absolutely, yes.

But it doesn't show anything really magical. What does indicate a magical happening, however, is when someone took the time to tell me how much they *loved* what I was doing.

While we were testing our collective butts off, I made it a habit to read every customer service email that we received, and there were hundreds of them every day. It's something a lot of young executives and CEOs don't do (and I think that's a mistake) because we got some of our best ideas for new features and site improvements that way.

Within the first week of reading all these emails, one particular email caught my attention. The email started by thanking me for building AYI, because this person used it and realized a friend was also using it. She clicked on him, and they made a match. She went on to say they started joking around about whether or not they really liked each other. It turns out they had secretly liked each other for many years, but never had the guts to tell each other about it.

That was such a fun and rewarding email for me to read. Not only did it support my thought that my app was helping people to find matches and live better lives, but it also reinforced my suspicion that we were onto something magical. No other dating site at the time could tap into a friend's network to see potential matches or to leverage the ability to meet new friends.

#ExplosiveGrowthTip 23: Read all your customer emails, because there's a pot of gold in them if you look closely enough. If you have too many customer emails to review, have somebody summarize them each week for you, but never become disconnected from your customer. Did you read all your customer service emails last month?

THIS COULD BE MAGIC ON STEROIDS

Building off the positive vibes I got from that email, I went back to my belief that if I could make an action that users are already trying to do much easier for them (10X easier), I would have a winning product or feature.

I figured we could make it easier for the user to find potential matches among friends by adding a filter that only browsed a user's friends list, instead of friends randomly appearing within thousands of other search results. The concept of getting any kind of match was a magical moment for the user, but the idea of getting a match with a friend was magic on steroids. It provided us with the Holy Grail for products, which is when users talk about your product with friends offline. Word of mouth is free advertising, which is a tremendous advantage. This innovation inspired people to start conversations like, "Hey, I clicked "yes" on you on AYI last night, and guess what? We're a match! Isn't that funny? Wait...so, what do you think about that sort of thing? I mean it's not such a crazy idea, is it?"

The steroid effect got bigger. Think Mark McGwire when he was with the Oakland A's, as opposed to his days with the Cardinals, when he was allegedly injecting enough androstenedione to make Mickey Mouse look like Mike Tyson. We applied the "matching with friends" concept to our A/B testing of incentivizing users: we offered users the chance to see which of their friends liked them by inviting twenty friends, and it worked spectacularly.

MAKING AYI TEN, A HUNDRED, AND A THOUSAND TIMES BETTER

One characteristic shared by a lot of great products throughout history is it takes something people are already doing and makes it much easier or better. It's the 10X factor I mentioned previously. AYI addressed all the major pain points of IMFT.

The user could establish a complete profile, including pictures and any other key information with just one click that imported their Facebook profile. Also, we were able to make the user's profile actively update along with their Facebook one. This meant no stale profiles, which is a common problem on all dating sites. No other dating site could provide that functionality. It's difficult to put an exact number on it, but AYI wasn't just incrementally better; it was massively better.

Resting on our laurels at that point would have been an understandable reaction, but not smart. We knew we needed to put the pedal to the metal, continue to innovate, and try to make AYI a hundred or even a thousand times better than anything else.

When you work as closely with another company as we did with Facebook, many people think you're the same company, or you're at least affiliated with them somehow. At the time, Facebook limited the number of friends a user could add, and we started to get Facebook's complaint emails about that limitation. Not only did I realize that meant they cared about both websites, but it also inspired another idea.

I thought, "People are adding friends on Facebook after connecting with them on our app. Why don't we make that a lot easier for them?" So, we built a feature that allowed users to click on an AYI user, and send them a friend request on Facebook. At that point, we were trying to make money as a company (rather than merely surviving like we had for the first few years), so we charged for that feature, and it proved to be a very profitable add-on for us.

By adding features that users liked and couldn't be found anywhere else, we became known as one of the most forward-thinking companies in the industry. That distinction was mostly a result of just having my ear to the ground and listening to our users' wants and likes. By personally reading all the message boards and customer emails, I acquired a tremendous feel for how to continually improve our product and solve the problems of our customers. As we started implementing all those improvements, AYI went from ten times better to a hundred times better than anything that previously existed in the online dating world.

As companies grow, the decision makers and CEOs often become disconnected from their users, as layers of employees are hired to address issues. Ironically, the lowest paid employees (usually customer service reps) know the most about the user experience and what customers want, with no ability to follow up on problems or user feedback. Make sure you don't become disconnected from the users.

 #ExplosiveGrowthTip 24: Do you have *every* employee (including management) spend one hour per quarter with customer service, listening to calls and answering customer emails?

THE HOTTIE FEATURE

Another one of our most successful feature add-ons came from a seemingly innocuous conversation with one of our early engineers, Nazar. As we were testing a different feature and we were browsing profiles on the app, I made an observation: "How come every profile that comes up is a beautiful woman with blonde hair and blue eyes?"

He replied, "I don't want to tell you, because you'll get angry."

I said calmly, "I don't get angry...almost never, in fact."

He sheepishly responded, "Cliff, we have a lot of users. Some of them aren't the most attractive people in the world, and I happen to really appreciate physical beauty in women. So, I built a feature that only shows me attractive women when I'm browsing the profiles."

I paused, gave it some thought, overlooked the obvious interpretation of shallowness, and responded, "You're a genius!"

My next question was, "How does it work?"

He said, "It's pretty simple really. I determine attractiveness by simply finding out how often a user gets liked as opposed to how often they are skipped. Based on that, I created a filter that only shows me the profiles of women with the highest like-to-skip ratio."

Immediately, I decided to implement that filter as an add-on we could charge our users for. We called it "The Hottie Feature," and it made a lot of money for us as well.

#ExplosiveGrowthTip 25: Try to hire employees who will also use your product, because they will have some of the best ideas and will outperform non-user employees. Do at least 20 percent of your employees use the product regularly?

THE BEST IDEAS CAN COME FROM STRANGE PLACES

Just like inspiration, genius can also come from some of the strangest places. The Hottie Feature ended up being a big moneymaker, and it was discovered because I happened to randomly work with an engineer, and was emotionally invested enough to ask a harmless question based on what I saw.

That situation was typical—our best ideas wouldn't necessarily come from the people who were getting paid a lot of money to come up with them. I recognized how a customer email and an engineer who had no knowledge of online dating inspired or designed features that were beyond anything I was thinking about when I started the company.

Once I realized how great ideas could come from strange places, I decided to hold regular brainstorming sessions at monthly, company-wide meetings, where anyone with an idea for any of our products could share it for potential implementation.

#ExplosiveGrowthTip 26: Hold a monthly brainstorm session, ideally with a theme such as "new features" or a specific goal and encourage the entire company to participate. Did you have a brainstorm meeting with all of the company's participation recently?

KICK 'EM WHEN THEY'RE DOWN

Even more important than becoming experts on Facebook virality and feature implementation was site optimization. We needed to make sure that our site not only performed well, but that it stayed up and didn't suffer any serious problems with lag time.

At any given moment, AYI could have had tens or hundreds of thousands of users on it at once, which could have seriously bogged down performance. In those days, very few companies had experience dealing with so many users trying to simultaneously gain access, so this was a problem that required serious attention.

One of our competitors for space on Facebook at the time was a new app called Matches (not to be confused with the previously mentioned, out-of-touch-industry goliath, Match), that was growing like crazy. Due to the rapid growth, the app began to suffer from performance issues like frequent crashes. Eventually, the owner decided to take the app offline for a week to rewrite the code and ensure the new version could handle the traffic demands. It was a gamble, but I'm sure he realized they weren't going to be able to continue doing business with such stability issues. In a way, I had to admire his decisiveness and tenacity, taking the bull by the horns and addressing his issues with drastic measures. But I didn't think they could recover from being offline for a week. If we suffered the same fate at some point, we would have been finished as well.

We didn't have a lot of money left, and we were at a pivotal point in our business's survival. AYI needed to take advantage of our biggest competitor being offline—we needed to kick 'em while they were down. We also needed to ensure we didn't end up in the same situation. If ever there was a time to take a chance, this was it. I decided to hire an external site optimization firm to review and optimize our code so it could better handle the current and anticipated traffic. We paid a lot of money for this site optimization service, because the firm we hired was considered the best. My instructions were also very clear: we could not take the site down under any circumstances.

The investment paid off—our site never crashed. It stayed up and ran faster than ever. By the time the Matches app came back, we had acquired hundreds of thousands of users, and they never recovered. I truly believe if we had never made that big, somewhat risky investment, or if Matches had chosen to keep their app up and running (assuming they had the money to do it) while addressing their optimization issues, they would have gone on to enjoy the success that we did.

#ExplosiveGrowthTip 27: Better late than never is a bad plan for site reliability. Users are ruthless, and if your product doesn't work, they will go somewhere else, fast. Are you actively addressing site reliability?

The idea of knowing when to take a big risk and hiring the best when you need to assume that risk is one of the biggest lessons we learned as a company. I will repeat that action in another future business venture in a heartbeat if I have to.

CORPORATE BOUNTY HUNTERS

When an industry leader like Match (the out-of-touch-industry goliath this time) takes a shot at you in the press, that's one way to know you've arrived. However, when a company says they're fully committed to taking you down, that's an indicator that you've not only arrived, but you've shown up in a chauffeur-driven limousine, and you've been greeted by the paparazzi snapping pics to sell to the nearest tabloid for a front-page story.

Facebook wasn't always the behemoth it is today; it was a start-up once too, and had some rough edges that needed to be smoothed out. At first, there were no rules for apps on the platform. Apps could post to a user's wall and do a variety of things to spur growth. Of course, what happens when you give an entrepreneur an inch of freedom to grow is that they take a mile, and keep taking more until you have to slap their hands and tell them to stay out of the cookie jar. Apps took advantage of the no-rules atmosphere by bombarding Facebook with spam, spam, and more spam, leaving a cluttered interface and ultimately hurting the user experience.

Because there were no rules at first, several companies took opportunities for fast growth by implementing shady tactics, but I refused such a notion. I always asked myself, "Could I with a straight face justify any of our actions to investors or Facebook, while also arguing it helped the Facebook user experience?" If I laughed while making my case, I wouldn't do it.

SNAP Interactive would never engage in unethical practices that diminished the user experience, no matter what the perceived advantage was. We were a public company, so we had to be extremely careful about such activity, but that sort of behavior was also not at all representative of me as a person. I became an entrepreneur because I wanted to innovate to improve people's lives, not to become an unconscionably pesky, spam-crazy nuisance.

This position would prove to be crucial to our relationship with Facebook as we saw several competitors get completely banned over the years. We became a favorite of Facebook, eventually getting a spot on their "white list" of a select few dating sites allowed to market on their platform. It was very difficult for a new company to get that access, which was a major disadvantage for them.

Due to the less-than-scrupulous behavior of some of those apps, Facebook was forced to implement several rules and policies to limit the undesirable activities of some of the bad actors on the site. Unfortunately, it became a game of back-and-forth. Facebook would institute some rules to address one problem, and the bad actors would simply adjust tactics to continue their detrimental activity while staying within the bounds of acceptable behavior. The rules were changing constantly, and it was extremely difficult to keep up with them all. It would have been very easy to break one of them without even realizing it.

During this time of uneasiness, we attended a Facebook conference while AYI was one of the ten largest apps on Facebook, and the largest dating app. Our growth rocket had been officially launched and seemed to be moving at the speed of light. At the time, we were known as the group that had "figured out online dating," and were experts at leveraging virality to reach new heights of growth on Facebook.

At this conference, one of the higher-ups at Facebook pulled me aside and told me there was one very large company at the conference that was committed to taking other apps down. They had raised a massive amount of capital and were one of the biggest developers on the site, so they had the money and the power to do it.

Fortunately, we were considered one of the good guys on Facebook, because we did play by the rules. Because of that good relationship, we were communicating with the corporate leaders quite often, and they gave us a very useful heads-up in that particular situation.

That source went on to tell me that the company's strategy to eliminate competition was to report every instance of rules' violations to Facebook. Worse yet, they had a full-time new hire—a bounty hunter of sorts—whose sole mission was to take down SNAP Interactive.

My source told me that he knew it's extremely difficult to keep up with the constantly changing rules and policies, but if they got a report about something we were doing that wasn't in line with policy, they would have to take action. The actions they would take could be severe, such as taking our app completely offline—the equivalent of corporate homicide for us.

CORPORATE COPYCATS

"Imitation is the sincerest form of flattery."

—CHARLES CALEB COTTON, NINETEENTH-CENTURY ENGLISH WRITER AND CLERIC

SNAP Interactive was officially immersed in a cutthroat world of cunning competitors, hell-bent on our destruction, and corporate copycats, dedicated to shamelessly imitating our best features. Flattery or not, that form of imitation was a tough pill to swallow.

Hot or Not was our chief competitor at the time. We were the two largest dating apps, and at one point, we had talked about engaging in some business opportunities together, but they never happened. What did happen was they copied just about every viral growth implementation we came up with, even down to the same typos in the footer. Imitation is one thing, but this was downright cloning.

Hot or Not wasn't a newcomer copycat. They basically invented the online dating app and were the first real viral sensation. Their fascination with our features and brazen theft of our creativity was more likely an act of desperation than anything else. Their activity steadily declined, mostly because they were always two steps behind us. They didn't know we had released numerous iterations of our app due to our approach of constant testing. It was possible they were stuck running inferior versions of their copycatted features. Justice was eventually served; Hot or Not got desperate and sold, while AYI continued to grow.

That imitation game served as another striking realization for me: if one of the most famous and successful viral sites of the past several years thought we were so smart, so good, and so unique that they had to copy us to survive, we must be doing a lot of things really well.

 #ExplosiveGrowthTip 28: When a competitor starts

copying your features, you can pretty much write them off completely, as it means they ran out of innovative ideas. Are you copying features?

THE $10 MILLION CHECK I LEFT ON THE TABLE

As it turns out, we were definitely doing some things very well, but there were other things happening I wish I could have had a second chance at. If I knew then what I know now, maybe some defining moments would have gone down a little differently...or maybe not.

That uneasy feeling in the pit of your stomach that causes anxiety, agitation, and more than a few sleepless nights—that's what I think of when describing regret. It's a terrible feeling to live with if you let it get larger than your hope for the future, but that's not what successful entrepreneurs do. I'm not here to dwell on them (because I'm way past that), but as Sinatra said, *"Regrets...I've had a few."*[1]

In the midst of this period of explosive growth through Facebook, when some companies were gunning for us and others were blatantly ripping us off, a venture capitalist approached me with an offer that I couldn't refuse—but I did.

---

1   "My Way" written by Paul Anka, Claude Francois, and Jacques Revaux.

This venture capitalist asked me to fly out to Silicon Valley to meet with him, so I obliged him because this could have meant a whole lot of money coming our way. When I got there, he told me he thought what we were doing at SNAP Interactive was great—we had a great product, we were growing very fast, and they wanted to be part of it. He was willing to make a very large investment in our company, and he went on to discuss the details of how such an arrangement would work.

"Let's talk," he said. "With my investment, you'll become the largest dating site in the world. Based on what Match.com is currently worth, plus your projected growth, that would come out to a valuation of about $1 billion."

The idea was to accelerate our growth by using his investment capital to pay to acquire millions of users on Facebook. By doing that, it was easy to see how we could get to fifty or a hundred million users fast. It was a simple hypothesis, the math was solid, and I definitely agreed with how it would work.

"The terms are going to be great, but there is one stipulation: you have to agree to move to Silicon Valley and bring the company with you," he revealed.

I questioned him, "Why?"

"That's where all the top-tier Facebook engineering talent is, and I want you to be directly linked with that. There's no way a company in New York City can compete with a similar company in Silicon Valley," he said.

Unfortunately, I completely agreed with his logic. We got extremely lucky to have elite professionals like Mike Sherov and Jim Supple with us from the beginning, but it was very hard for us to find more talent—there weren't enough guys like them in our area to match the Silicon Valley talent pool.

I fully recognized that talent was everything in the tech world, but I also understood the roots of the key people who contributed so massively to the foundation and subsequent growth of my company. My brother Darrell (cofounder) and my father, both based in the New York area, had been heavily involved with the business from the beginning as well. There were also many other key employees to consider like Jim and Mike. In all likelihood, neither of them would move from their Long Island roots. It just didn't feel right.

Regretfully, I told the investor, "No, thank you."

"Just so you understand," he clarified, "I have a $10 million check in my pocket, and I'm going to give it to somebody today. It's yours if you want it, but if you don't, it's going to the next guy, who is already in Silicon Valley, which will instantly make them your biggest competitor."

I gave him my final answer. "I get it, but it's just not going to happen."

I never told anyone about that conversation. It seemed too risky—I thought it might spook people. I didn't want anyone to feel like they were on borrowed time in any way. It would have been very easy for people—even tremendously talented ones—to lose focus in that sort of working environment, so I kept it to myself for a long time.

Shortly thereafter, Zoosk (one of our biggest competitors) raised around $20 million in venture capital. They announced their growth plan, and it was unsettlingly similar to the conversation I'd had that day in Silicon Valley. Zoosk began spending money like drunken sailors on leave in a tropical island paradise. The company used their newfound wealth to acquire millions of users, which ultimately made them much larger than us.

What would have happened if I'd said yes that day instead? We certainly would have ventured down a different path. In the short-term, Zoosk became worth hundreds of millions of dollars, and at one point was on a path to having a massive

Initial Public Offering (IPO). They eventually struggled because their product wasn't as good as ours, but they're still around and have revenues several times larger than ours.

The funny thing is I regretted my decision to reject the $10 million almost as soon as the words came out of my mouth; taking the money would have been the best long-term decision for the company. But my employees were everything to me at that point. I didn't want to lose that connection and introduce a massive disruption while things were going so well.

My regret is that I didn't even explore the possibility of moving the company—I just squashed the idea on the spot like a bug. I could have shared my views with the employees, and perhaps they would have been open to moving. Even if they weren't flexible about moving, I at least would have explored the option and then could've have assured them we wouldn't be going anywhere.

GO AWAY, NOBODY'S HOME

Doing things my way always felt right, but that didn't mean my way couldn't be changed periodically. Every so often, something happened that made it abundantly clear I needed to change something, and sometimes, it was a big change.

Draw the curtains, shut off the lights, and don't answer the door or the phone. Be quiet everyone and stay away from the windows...That's what most of us say and do when an extreme religious organization comes to the front door, an annoying telemarketer calls, or the bill collector shows up.

Now, think of SNAP Interactive as the bill collector, and a very large, prominent ad network as the people hiding beneath the windows of their palatial estate in Silicon Valley. This ad network owed us $90,000 (nearly half of our total revenue for the month) and decided not to pay.

Two weeks before this nameless company decided to steal $90,000 worth of ad revenue from us, we had had a meeting with them where they assigned us to a personal account rep, and told us how valuable our relationship was to them. Two weeks later, all the niceties and gestures of goodwill ceased, along with any form of communication. We tried calling them to collect our money many times and got no response. They went radio silent.

This company had so much money that $90,000 to them was akin to about $10 for my company and about a nickel to the average American worker, so lack of money wasn't the reason for nonpayment. My suspicions told me that another very large dating site that we knew did a lot more business with that ad network than we did, and had bullied them into kicking us off the network. I could never prove anything like that, but that's the only explanation that made any sense to me.

AYI had been an ad-based revenue model (more on that in the next chapter). When this one client who made up nearly half of our monthly revenue decided not to pay, it was very troubling and eye-opening. We were already heavily dependent on the success of Facebook and their ability to deliver us millions of users. Having revenue stolen from us through corporate bullying—grand larceny might be a better term—showed me we were also too dependent on individual ad networks to pay us. I wondered what would happen to us if those ad networks either went bankrupt themselves or more of them just didn't pay us?

I concluded that we needed to gain more control of our own destiny. One way to do that was to change our revenue model from ad-based to subscription-based—but was that the right thing to do?

 #ExplosiveGrowthTip 29: If your largest source of revenue stopped paying you or disappeared, could your business survive for at least six months? Come up with a contingency plan now.

6

FROM REVENUES OF $3 MILLION TO $19 MILLION IN TWO YEARS!

"Timing, perseverance, and ten years of trying will eventually make you look like an overnight success."

—BIZ STONE, COFOUNDER OF TWITTER

By November 2009, SNAP Interactive had a well-known industry presence with AYI being the largest and most active dating app. It had a consistent ranking as a top five app overall on Facebook, even reaching number two at one point. We had over twenty million installs and several million monthly active users. However, we were still mired in a somewhat frustrating spot: numerous apps around us with similar or inferior metrics were either being valued at or sold for hundreds of millions of dollars. Yet, as a public company, we were still undiscovered.

Wall Street still wasn't giving us any credit for our growth and user metrics, and our company was valued at less than $10 million—not much more than a start-up with just an idea would be valued at. We tried to raise money, but went zero for one-hundred when we sought investors. That's right: we approached over one-hundred investors, and none of them offered us any sort of capital for various maddening reasons.

Since we were publicly traded, most venture capital firms were prohibited from investing in us, because their big payday is usually when a company turns public. That left us to approach public market investors, such as hedge funds. However, with the depressed valuation and the company trading on the OTC BB stock exchange (our valuation wasn't high enough to trade on the NASDAQ), most hedge funds weren't allowed to invest in us for legal reasons. We explored taking the company private, but that was an extremely complicated and involved process. Also working against us was the fact that Wall Street wasn't yet familiar with Facebook and its future prospects. We were truly stuck between a rock and a hard place.

Meanwhile, Zoosk had just raised a total of about $40 million in venture capital, and Zynga (an online gaming platform) had raised $50 million. With competitors having pockets that deep to spend on user acquisition, marketing, and gold-plated, championship foosball tables if they desired, we were at a big disadvantage. Continuing to grow virally at that point had become quite difficult, so we had to do something else to even the playing field.

Our ad-based revenue model wasn't helping our situation, because the amount we got paid varied by as much as 50 percent depending on the market for that day. When the market got cold, our revenue dropped substantially. Also, if our site went down for as little as two hours, we would lose around 10 percent of our revenue for that day. Although we had experienced terrific and profitable growth in just two years, the revenue had stagnated after the first year, growing just five percent from 2008 to 2009. It wasn't clear how revenues were going to explode from here—and that's what investors wanted to see.

YEAR	REVENUES ($000)	ANNUAL INCREASE
2007	$425	NA
2008	$3,012	609%
2009	$3,171	5%

FROM ADS TO SUBSCRIPTIONS

"Subscribers are better than customers."

—JOHN WARRILLOW, AUTHOR OF *THE*
AUTOMATIC CUSTOMER: CREATING A
SUBSCRIPTION BUSINESS IN ANY INDUSTRY

We needed to change the way we made money. We wanted to control our own destiny and an ad-based revenue model wasn't predictable enough. The obvious choice was a subscription-based revenue model, which was already a common approach in the online dating space.

Subscriptions are very consistent and predictable, and they enable accurate revenue forecasting and cash flow many months out. Knowing that recurring future revenue is certain provides confidence to invest in the business today. The days of losing half of our revenue because one client decided not to pay us would be over, and even the site going down wouldn't affect subscriptions.

Moving from ads to subscriptions would be no problem, right? Wrong. We were already established as a completely free service. How could I tell our users, "Hey, thanks for using our online dating app while it was free. How about paying us ten, twenty, or maybe thirty dollars per month from now on to use the same damned thing?"

THE TESTING

Going guns blazing at our existing user base like that would have been remarkably stupid—the 10X effect of stupid—and we all knew that. We knew we needed to tread carefully, so we implemented our new revenue model methodically after rigorous testing for about three months. But was that enough?

We started testing in our second largest market, the UK, and implemented a few different messaging models. After that amount of time, we measured the impact on revenue and users from such a change. The data made it abundantly clear that although usage dropped quickly, the revenue immediately more than doubled from the initial subscriptions, even before the impact of the recurring subscriptions.

We believed that the triple-digit increase in revenue would enable us to acquire users even more quickly through paid user acquisition. This would now allow us to compensate for any short-term drop in user growth and usage due to users having to suddenly pay for the service. Ultimately, we viewed it as a hugely successful test result, so we ran with it.

Anticipating the ability to hire more staff and achieve triple-digit revenue growth, we unveiled our subscription model to the whole system. After that, we expected investors to line up at our doorstep as if they were waiting outside the box office for tickets to see Lady Gaga unveil her newest meat suit in concert.

THE RESULTS

Initially, our forecasts proved to be correct: our revenue exploded, growing for twelve straight quarters from $3 million to $19 million annually (a truly phenomenal performance by any measure), which gained us many awards and notoriety. We truly achieved explosive growth from a revenue perspective with this methodical change.

YEAR	REVENUE ($000)	ANNUAL INCREASE	INCREASE SINCE 2007
2007	$425	NA	NA
2008	$3,012	609%	609%
2009	$3,171	5%	646%
2010	$6,669	110%	1,469%
2011	$19,156	187%	4,407%
2012	$19,247	0%	4,429%

DOWN 90 PERCENT

As our revenue grew, our usage declined steadily to around 50 percent, which we fully expected because of the data we got from the testing phase in the UK. This didn't send us into a state of panic, because our plan was to use the increase in revenues to increase our marketing spend on user acquisition. We felt this would more than offset any initial traffic declines due to charging users. However, certain metrics then plummeted as far down as 90 percent in some geographies. This was definitely a wake-up call, even though the revenues were truly exploding. Equally as unexpected was that after some initially sustained growth, revenue began to decline as well a few years later.

With decreasing usage came a decreasing quality of user experience. Suddenly, the network effect was working against us. What's the point of paying even ten dollars per month for a dating service that doesn't have a steady influx of new profiles to view? The negative effects continued. Users became upset at being charged for a service they were accustomed to getting for free, and who could blame them?

In the app world, reviews are everything. Many potential users will base their entire purchase decision on the reviews. Not only did we get numerous scathing reviews from angry users on Facebook, but we also got a lot of negative reviews from our newly released iOS app. We were getting publicly beaten down like an intoxicated, shirtless fan running onto the field at Yankee Stadium.

WHAT DID WE LEARN?

In hindsight, we learned a few things from this experience:

- 💣 We didn't have a long enough sample size for our testing to show us how the change in revenue model would affect the company over the long term. Although we tested the model for three months, we should have given it about a six- to nine-month trial run before releasing it system wide.

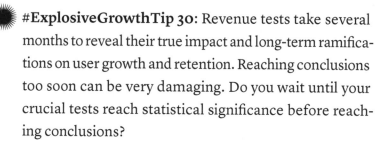 **#ExplosiveGrowthTip 30:** Revenue tests take several months to reveal their true impact and long-term ramifications on user growth and retention. Reaching conclusions too soon can be very damaging. Do you wait until your crucial tests reach statistical significance before reaching conclusions?

- 💣 You can't charge an existing user base a monthly subscription for something they've already been using for free. It's going to result in anger, poor reviews, and a bad relationship with users. It proved something I mentioned earlier: if they hated us, they must have cared.

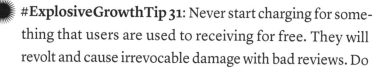 **#ExplosiveGrowthTip 31:** Never start charging for something that users are used to receiving for free. They will revolt and cause irrevocable damage with bad reviews. Do

you have any plans to charge for features you are currently giving away for free?

- 💣 We should have brainstormed a little more about how to more wisely implement the change. If we thought about it long enough, we would have realized we could have charged for new and advanced features, while leaving the basic service free.

#ExplosiveGrowthTip 32: Come up with new features to charge users for instead of monetizing previously free features.

Book Recommendation: *The Automatic Customer: Creating a Subscription Business in Any Industry* by John Warrillow.

"THE DILDO AND VIBRATOR ARE NOT ACCEPTABLE"

Businesses are always looking for ways to increase revenues, and getting existing customers to pay more money (usually for new features) is much easier than acquiring new users. This is referred to as increasing your lifetime value (LTV) per customer.

When we implemented the subscription model, the LTV of a customer was capped at around twenty dollars a month.

Virtual gifts provided a way for us to substantially increase our LTV per customer and recover financially.

Virtual gifts were images of objects people could send to each other online through messages. They were things like roses, money, diamond rings, gold bars, cars, or anything else. They were becoming popular in any sort of messaging app at that time, but hadn't made their way into the dating space until we introduced them.

Virtual gifts in our apps were mostly used by guys looking for that one nuanced thing to separate themselves from the pack of drooling hounds chasing attractive women online. Most guys would send relatively cheap virtual gifts (like flowers costing a few dollars), but the expensive ones, such as the fifty-dollar gold bar certainly indicated a different level of disposable income and sincere interest—exactly what the girls were looking for. Once we realized this, we included in plain text exactly how much the virtual gift cost—right on the message that came with it.

With virtual gifts, the "whales" (people who wanted to spend a lot of money to stand out from the crowd) could spend unlimited amounts of money on top of the monthly subscription rate, thus increasing our revenues and LTV per user.

Virtual gifts were used in a game of who could spend more money than the next guy. Psychologically, this virtual contest between guys everywhere made all the sense in the world. Guys have been trying to impress women with jewelry, sports cars, luxury hotels, and everything else their income can afford them for centuries. Why wouldn't it extend to the virtual world as well?

Interestingly enough, there were still some men in Middle Eastern countries who were spending thousands of dollars on virtual gifts, usually the gold bars.

Around that same time, there was a Facebook app called Naughty Gifts, created by a successful entrepreneur named Adam Gries. It was mostly for people who wanted to send inappropriate images to friends for a laugh, and it was a tremendous success. Adam describes his inspiration for Naughty Gifts as follows:

> "I was inspired to start Naughty Gifts by a then-popular virtual gifting app called Free Gifts, created by Zach Allia. The viral opportunity was that a user could send a gift to twenty friends at once. Facebook would inform the recipient about the gift, and they then had to download the app to view the gift. I believed that taking an application that was already working (Free Gifts), tweaking it for a highly resonant sub-segment,

and giving it a provocative name (Naughty Gifts) would likely be a winner. It was obvious to me that offering a virtual naughty gift would be like crack. Just imagine your response to the notification, 'Adam sent you a gift, click here to see what it is.' vs. 'Adam sent you a *naughty* gift, click here to see what it is.' Bottom line, just like anything else: sex sells and curiosity is fuel to the fire. Within a couple of months, we had many millions of users, got massive press, including the *New York Times*, and we sold the app due to its massive scale.

We pondered the possibility of integrating such a feature into our virtual gifts. However, we were still cognizant that we were being watched closely by that unnamed company for any possible infraction of Facebook's rules and policies.

Being a proactive company rather than reactive, we decided to get in front of any possible problems by contacting Facebook to find out what images would be deemed acceptable and which ones would be unacceptable. We sent them an email with a bunch of images (things like boxers, bras, or other risqué items like handcuffs or masks) asking, "Can you please let us know which images are okay to use and which ones are not?" One of my favorite emails ever came back from the Facebook policy team articulately stating, "Most of these images are fine, including the handcuffs and the bull whip. However, I'm afraid that the dildo and the vibrator are not acceptable. Thanks for checking!"

HELLO, MARK CUBAN

Even though our usage took a big hit from the change in revenue model, we still had explosive revenue numbers, because we still had a great user experience, and we were constantly adding new features that users loved. Also, the stock was really cheap (late December of 2010 was still a few months away). Although Wall Street was still ignoring us, we were well known and unique within the Facebook community. To the savvy investor, we were probably a pretty good buy at that point.

Speaking of savvy investors, one day I looked through the list of stockholders and spotted Mark Cuban's name among our largest shareholders. That was a really exciting discovery for me. He never contacted us, so we had no idea he was a shareholder until that moment. I reached out to him, and we ended up having discussions about working together. He had some ideas for new apps he wanted us to build. I turned Mark Cuban down, just like I'd turned down the venture capitalist with a big check burning a hole in his pocket.

Around the same time, I was introduced to some other superstar entrepreneurs, such as bestselling authors Tim Ferriss and Gary Vaynerchuk (who both asked about joining our board of directors).

Everything was moving so fast, but one thing I always wanted to maintain as an entrepreneur was my focus. I turned down Cuban, Ferriss, and Vaynerchuk because I didn't want to lose focus on my niche in the online dating space. Cuban's app wasn't a dating app, and I was very concerned about spreading myself and my development resources too thin. There was a lot going on at the time—worrying about corporate bounty hunters, copycats, changing revenue models, and managing our growing company. I always said to myself, "If I'm going to screw this thing up, it's not going to be from a lack of focus."

Now that I have had a chance to look back on everything, I realize that turning down a billionaire and a couple of entrepreneurial legends was a mistake. But, I'm going to take that lesson forward with me to my next entrepreneurial endeavor. I can always take solace in knowing I still did what I thought was right at the time.

THE BILLIONAIRE RULE

Do I regret not working with Mark Cuban?

Yes.

Do I regret not welcoming Tim Ferriss and Gary Vayner-chuk onto the board of directors?

Affirmative, once again.

My mistake in turning down those opportunities was not realizing another very important rule of successful entrepreneurism, which is the following:

"We are the average of the five people we spend the most time with."

—JIM ROHN, MOTIVATIONAL SPEAKER

#ExplosiveGrowthTip 33: Write down the five people you spend the most time with. If you become the average of them, would you be happy with that outcome? If not, it might be time to upgrade your inner circle.

Cross-reference that thought to the chance to work with guys like Cuban, Ferriss, and Vaynerchuk, and if those were three of the five people I was surrounded by, I would have been in very good company. To be fair, it's unclear how much time would have been spent with any of them, because a board member's direct involvement can vary greatly. However, it was shortsighted of me not to realize that surrounding myself with the smartest and most successful people I knew could have led to better results. Perhaps one of them would have become my mentor and helped me ultimately fulfill my dream of being an NBA general manager or owner (Hello, Mark Cuban?).

A few years too late, my good friend and mentor, Andrew, explained to me something he calls The Billionaire Rule, which is: *Any time a billionaire wants to work with you, never say, "No."*

#ExplosiveGrowthTip 34: When a billionaire wants to work with you, never say no. Are you fully exploring opportunities to work with a billionaire?

I wish I would have looked a little deeper into a possible working relationship with those three superstar entrepreneurs. Was it a big mistake, however, to choose focusing on my core business over branching out into areas of unfamiliarity? I'm not so sure about that. The optimal choice would have likely been to keep brainstorming about how to create something that would align with everyone's interests, while maintaining a focus on my core business.

MY $78 MILLION WEEK

"A million dollars isn't cool. You know what's cool? A billion dollars."

—SEAN PARKER IN *THE SOCIAL NETWORK*

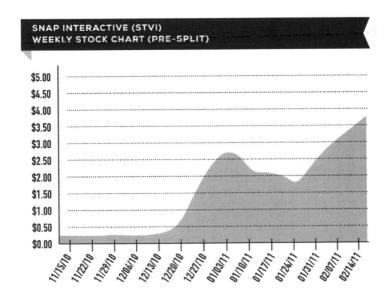

SNAP INTERACTIVE (STVI)
WEEKLY STOCK CHART (PRE-SPLIT)

The reporter from Bloomberg News called us in September of 2010 and said, "You guys are either the best undiscovered public company on Wall Street, or there's something amiss with your numbers. I would love to write a story on you, or at least come in and get down and dirty with your business to see if there's a story to be told."

I said, "Absolutely, we'd love to have you come in."

When he arrived that day at our office, we gave him full access to anything he wanted, including our employees and data. He spent several hours talking with everyone, examined all our numbers to ensure their legitimacy, and left without much fanfare. Then he disappeared for three months. We never heard from him again until December 22—the day our growth truly began to explode.

That was the day he called to ask us if we moved operations to a garage somewhere, the story that started this book.

That was the day before the article titled, "Facebook Friends in Search of Romance Drive Growth of Dating Application" came out and called us "the future of dating" and "an undiscovered gem of a public company."

That was the day before Greg Blatt, CEO of Match.com,

referred to us in that article as "a fun, flirty, little app with a few people working out of a garage."

That was the day before our stock rose from $0.20 to $0.50 per share, before skyrocketing to $3.20 on December 29, an increase of 1,500 percent. Ultimately, the stock hit its highest point of $4.50 at midday on February 15, 2011, making my personal net worth greater than $100 million.

Finally, December 22 was the day that began my $78 million week.

TIMING IS EVERYTHING

A month prior to the article that spurred our explosive growth, another article came out in a different online publication called the PE Hub, which is a very popular read in Silicon Valley and the investment community. The article was strikingly similar to the one that changed everything just a month later (and was the right audience too), but it didn't budge the needle. In fact, our stock didn't trade at all from it.

Therefore, when we first saw the article in Bloomberg News, we didn't think much of it. In fact, we had given up hope that a press article could do much of anything for our business at that point. It really wasn't until Maria

Bartiromo called, and we saw Business Insiders like Henry Blodget jumping on board that we realized something special might have been happening.

If both the PE Hub article and the one from Bloomberg News had essentially the same content with similarly targeted audiences, what was the big difference?

Once again, timing proved to be everything.

PE Hub published their article on an ordinary day in November, followed by another ordinary day in November, and so on. The Bloomberg News article, however, ran on Thursday, December 23, which coincided with the market being closed for the next three days. That closure allowed our stock story to gain increasing momentum each day, as the news continued to circulate in the minds of savvy investors everywhere until Wall Street opened again on Monday, December 27.

The best way to go completely viral is to do something that nobody else is doing, do it well, and if the timing is right—Boom! Explosive growth is the result. In our case, we had a uniquely intuitive and simple approach to online dating. We became known as the "Facebook Play" in the financial world. And, our timing was right, because the story of our fast-growing and unique product filled an empty news cycle for several days.

A HUNDRED REJECTIONS: HOW DO YOU LIKE US NOW?

Around the same time that the PE Hub article came out was when we approached over a hundred investors for a potential investment—and they all said no. During the week of the Bloomberg News article, just about every one of those same investors called me, trying to sell their souls for a piece of the pie. Even though they had all flat out turned us down when the company was valued around $8 million, now they wanted to jump in with the company valued at ten times that amount.

Goldman Sachs practically had me on speed dial and so did numerous financial publications around the country, trying to get more information about our company. They asked questions like, "How many employees do you have?" I would answer them, "Oh, we've got twelve." They would respond with, "Twelve hundred?" I would have to correct them every time, "No, just twelve, period." Then, I would start naming everyone: Darrell, Jim, Mike S, Mike W, Kim, Wei, Nazar, Olivia, etc., because with only twelve people, it was easy to know everyone's name.

With investors and giant financial firms falling at our feet like fifteen-year-old girls at a One Direction concert, we leveraged our moment in the spotlight for a very favorable capital raise. Previously, we would get a call or two per week, and jump on it right away. Now, the calls were coming so fast and furious that we were rerouting them to our lawyers to keep up with the demand. Goldman freakin' Sachs was calling us!

The company was experiencing high double-digit revenue growth, and we were suddenly profitable. Until that point, my best practice was to raise money from the people who believed in us from the beginning: friends and family. People who would also stay out of our way. That way, we didn't have any hot-shot venture capitalists controlling our destiny. However, I learned from my regrets—turning down Mark Cuban, Tim Ferriss, and Gary Vaynerchuk, and the venture capitalist who wanted us to move to the Valley. I should have given them all more consideration before making a decision. With all that in mind, I decided I should at least see if there was an irrefutable opportunity waiting.

TOXIC AVENGERS

I made some phone calls to banks of all sizes, while keeping an open mind at all times to what they had to offer us. Unfortunately, their list of demands came quicker than anything else:

- "You're going to have to do road shows." (Road shows are presentations to potential investors.)

- "It's going to take us a few weeks."
- "You're going to have to give up some board seats."

I just didn't have the time or will to listen to all the bull-shit doublespeak. I was putting in twelve-hour days at a minimum, seven days a week, sitting side-by-side with the programmers, trying to collaborate constantly on how we could keep growing faster than our competitors.

I told the banks, "I'll give you two days of my time. See if you can raise money for us in those two days at some-where around these specified stock prices. I know what I'm doing. I don't want to talk to investors, and I'm sure as hell not giving up one board seat." That deterred every bank we talked to, except one.

That banker said to me, "We can do this. Give me a two-week exclusivity, and we'll get this thing done."

I said, "Okay, but I'm not bluffing. You can't have two weeks either. I'll give you two days of my time. That's the best I can do."

A gentleman from that bank was in our office later that afternoon. We spent two days on a road show talking nonstop with investors (much to my chagrin, because most of the conversations with these investment professionals involved explaining concepts around technology that most third graders of today have a full grasp of). The questions were something like:

- 💣 "So, what is this Facebook app you're talking about?"
- 💣 "Explain to me what a newsfeed is again?"
- 💣 "Wait, I thought we were talking about a website. What's the difference between a website and an app exactly?"

Fortunately, explaining these rudimentary items over and over again was well worth my time, because interest among these Facebook newbies was absolutely through the roof. Just like they promised, they were not your typical investors. They weren't interested in board seats that I wasn't about to give away. The only thing they really wanted was to go along for the ride on a promising company whose stock was suddenly in high demand.

The deal progressed very quickly—a little too quickly for my comfort. I received all the paperwork on New Year's Eve, and I spent the evening reviewing hundreds of pages of legal material. We were just about to close the deal. The pen was hovering above the paper, ready to endorse a potential deal with the devil that could have had SNAP Interactive burning in the fiery pits of financial hell for eternity. But then I freaked out, which turned out to be a good thing.

As I flipped through the deluge of documents, I noticed an overflow of foreign terms that I knew nothing about. My attorneys were encouraging me to sign the papers, but they weren't giving me adequate explanations about the potential ramifications of the terms. Those terms ended up being more than just foreign—they were toxic. Although I didn't realize how dangerous they were at the time, I followed my gut, which was telling me if I didn't completely understand the magnitude of the contract, I needed to put the pen down and walk away, regardless of what everybody else was telling me to do.

"A FUCKING MORON!"

So, that's what I did. I put the pen down and called the banker. I said, "No deal. I have to understand what's in these documents before I sign anything. I'm not going to jeopardize my company just to rush through the closing of this deal."

That wasn't received very well. A lot of screaming and cursing went over the telephone lines that evening.

They said, "You were a worthless, shitty penny stock just a week ago. All you have to do is sign, and you'll have millions in the bank, while only giving up 10 percent of the company. This is the deal of a lifetime!"

I tried to interject, but was abruptly shouted down. Instead, they carried on, in a near hysterical manner, "You're a fucking moron! Just sign the fucking papers, because you don't have time to wait!" Without taking a breath, they escalated to confrontational, bullying tactics. "I'm coming to your apartment right now, and you're going to sign those papers."

Around 1:00 a.m., I heard from the Long Island banker (no knock on the door, fortunately). He called to say he was coming to NYC right away to "talk some sense into me." He said that he would meet me anywhere I wanted, but time could not be wasted.

Despite their threatening and bordering-on-assault objections, I flat out said, "I'm not going to sign anything under this kind of pressure. I'm out."

The cursing resumed for a little longer until they finally gave up, and the deal—as it was currently constituted—was off.

LET'S MAKE A DEAL...FINALLY!

Thank God, I rejected that deal, because it turns out that several of those onerous terms would have ultimately put us out of business several times over.

#ExplosiveGrowthTip 35: Don't be pressured into making any decisions or signing any documents you're unsure about. Rushing into a poor decision or agreement can be catastrophic, whereas missing an opportunity will not be.

Toxic terms were all over that document like ticks sucking the blood from a lazy basset hound laying in the woods. They acted as resets, which meant I could have been screwed if I ever needed to raise money again. That level of toxicity in a business deal is actually fairly typical for desperate companies, but that wasn't us.

I spent the next week or more going through the documents with a fine-toothed comb. I made the necessary changes to the legal documents, and in the meantime, the stock price not only held up, but it went even higher. The best part was that none of the investors cared that the toxic terms were removed, because we had a very promising and exciting business they were to be part of. We had all the leverage.

#ExplosiveGrowthTip 36: Leverage is everything in a negotiation. Understand when you have it and when you don't. Are you maximizing your leverage before key negotiations?

#ExplosiveGrowthTip 37: The best time to raise money

is when you don't need to. Is the company financially stable enough where you can walk away from a bad or mediocre term sheet?

Book recommendation: *Bargaining for Advantage: Negotiation Strategies for Reasonable People,* by G. Richard Shell.

At that time, we were growing by 50,000 new users per day, and we thought we were going to be the largest dating site in the world. The deal finally closed on January 14, and we raised $8.5 million at $2 per share, plus some warrants, which was the equivalent of an $80 million valuation. Think about that. In a span of just three weeks, our valuation increased by ten times, and we were able to raise more money at that valuation than our company was even worth several weeks earlier. The real kicker was that the money was coming from a lot of the same investors who wouldn't touch us just a few weeks prior.

We actually could have raised a lot more, because every few minutes a new group of investors wanted to get in on the deal. But we shut down the process at $8.5 million, because we didn't want to dilute ourselves too much, and that was already ten times more cash than we had ever had before.

 #ExplosiveGrowthTip 38: Investors are a lot like jealous exes—they want you a lot more when someone else is interested.

FOCUS, PLEASE

Those days were really interesting times around our office. We were getting press coverage and stock inquiries like we were a biotech company that had discovered a way of cooking bacon to cure cancer. It was hard to remain focused, but overall, I think we managed it really well.

How did we keep our heads down and our collective noses to the grindstone amidst such revelry? I think the company followed my lead.

Everyone saw how I responded to all the insanity going on around us—in the news, on Wall Street, and even in the office. The staff would hear that a million different television producers were trying to fly me to La-La Land for an appearance on a talk show. Goldman Sachs was desperately trying to reach me, as well as a gaggle of other financial firms and high-powered individual investors. My response was usually something like, "Gee, I'm kind of busy today, Mr. Buffett, or should I call you Warren? There's a very important product meeting this afternoon that's going to take up a lot of my day, but I might have a small window between 3:00 and 3:15, if you're free.

Other than that, it could be a few weeks before we can get together."

Some looked at me like I was crazy. Others just laughed and shook their heads. It didn't matter what their reaction was, because the message got through loud and clear: nothing had changed.

We needed to keep innovating, outworking everybody else, and above all, staying focused. None of those things should change just because Goldman Sachs and Maria Bartiromo were calling. That was my message, but despite my best efforts to keep everyone focused and maintain the status quo, some things changed anyway.

FROM STUPID TO SMART IN ONE DAY

Around the time when we were being rejected by all those investors, everyone questioned why we went public so soon with the self-registration. Investors were completely ignoring us, because they thought our company was worthless. I think some people viewed us as the dumbest company on Wall Street in those days.

That all changed during my $78 million week. All of a sudden, going public was seen as a gesture of genius instead of a stroke of *stoopid*. Everyone around me—

friends, relatives, and mere acquaintances—were all treating me differently than ever before. Even my dating life had changed, and I needed to accept some new challenges in that aspect of my life as well.

SMALL FORTUNES FOR FRIENDS AND FAMILY

Several of the original investors who were friends and family members made small fortunes, some making nearly fifty times their original investment. One of them used their gains to go back to school and get an advanced degree, while others used the money to buy new homes. Years later, one friend told me that his $5,000 investment had made him over $100,000, and he used it to pay for his wedding and honeymoon. I responded, "The least you could have done was invite me to the wedding."

There was a woman I had been pursuing for a long time. One night, she finally agreed to go out to dinner with me. Halfway through the dinner, she said, "Can I ask you something?"

I replied, "Sure, you can ask me anything you want."

She said, "My friend works on Wall Street, and he said you're worth about $100 million. Is that true?"

Somewhat taken by surprise (and more than a little disappointed), I responded, "On paper, I guess I am worth close to $100 million. So that's true."

Later that evening, I politely declined an invitation to her place—having been entirely turned off by her painfully shallow question. I realized everybody's perception of me and my company had changed. Now, I had to adjust my expectations, my approach to work, and my personal life to meet those changes.

Another thing I noticed was that suddenly, everybody seemed to think that every idea I had was absolutely brilliant. At any given moment, I could storm out of my office and declare through a circus-sized megaphone, "From now on, everybody needs to come to work wearing their underwear on the outside of their pants!" I have no doubt that people would have responded quite positively to my newest form of brilliant tyranny, "Great idea, boss man—absolutely genius! I'm going to do that right now."

Fortunately for the company and staff, tyranny was never part of my game plan or personal makeup, so I never truly tested the waters with this totalitarian position. But that lack of resistance, pushback, or any questioning of my authority posed a real problem.

Nobody wanted to step up and challenge my ideas anymore. I didn't even need to know what the hell I was talking about half the time, and people just nodded their heads and did my bidding without questioning my idea's validity. It happens all the time when people achieve a certain level of success. They get way too much credit, even if the idea is totally out of their area of expertise or just plain ridiculous. It was very frustrating and confusing to me, because I didn't want people to be afraid to tell me that an idea I had was bad. It's nearly impossible to get valid feedback that way.

DON'T LET IT (ALL) RIDE

Fortunately, my perceived power never ran amuck or led to any harmful corporate chaos, because I became well aware of the problem that my lack of constructive feedback and questioning of my actions could pose. However, that didn't mean I wasn't susceptible to other mistakes typical of young successful entrepreneurs.

One of those mistakes was that I let it all (the money) ride. Risks are necessary to achieve truly impactful success, but one still needs to be smart. My advice to other young entrepreneurs in similar situations is to temper those risks with sound decision making.

At only thirty-two years old, I was worth around $100 million on paper, but I hadn't cashed any of that in yet. I always believed very strongly in what we were doing, and I honestly thought SNAP Interactive was going to be worth $1 billion someday, so why cash out on the cheap?

When we raised the $8.5 million, the bankers told me they would never be able to sell the deal if I tried to take some money off the table. They claimed that would indicate a lack of confidence in the company. I should have been able to sell some of my shares to new investors, which would take a few million dollars off the table. But I didn't, because the bankers told me I couldn't, which was not true.

The smart play would have been to challenge the bankers' refusal of my desire to take a few million dollars off the table when I had the chance. I was single with no kids to feed and no real responsibilities that I couldn't readily walk away from if I needed to. I figured I didn't need a whole lot of money to live, anyway. Plus, I thought to myself, "Why sell now when the company is going to be worth so much more later on?" That notion, however, was a bit of youthful foolishness on my part. I didn't need to let it *all* ride. I could have let *most* of it ride.

At its all-time high, SNAP Interactive's stock was worth $4.50 (Note: the stock has split since then, so comparisons to today's prices aren't relevant without factoring in the splits). That valued the company around $160 million at the time, with my personal stake being worth around $110 million. Unfortunately, I never pocketed any of that, and I should have. There's a little more on this multi-million-dollar *faux pas* of mine in the final chapter.

#ExplosiveGrowthTip 39: Whenever you can take some money off the table (especially life-changing money) do it.

Book Recommendation: *The Richest Man in Babylon,* by George S. Clason.

What I learned in hindsight was that people are driven by their own incentives, however major or minor they may seem to the rest of us. Would it have been tougher to sell a deal if I took $2-4 million off the table? Sure, but I'm confident it could have been done. We were in the driver's seat, and nearly every investor we spoke to ended up investing. Besides that, the stock actually continued to gain momentum and increased for several months after the deal (which is very unusual). It was, however, easier for the bankers to bully me into believing them when they told me that taking some money off the table wasn't an option.

8

SUCCESSFUL ON THE OUTSIDE, SCRAMBLING ON THE INSIDE

"However beautiful the strategy, you should occasionally look at the results."

—SIR WINSTON CHURCHILL, PRIME MINISTER OF THE
UNITED KINGDOM FROM 1940-1945 AND 1951-1955

Almost exactly one year after the Bloomberg News article ignited the fire on our stock's value, we rang the opening bell for NASDAQ on December 27, 2011. A lot had happened to SNAP Interactive in the 365 days leading up to that point:

- SNAP Interactive was ranked the thirty-sixth Fastest Growing Company in North America on Deloitte's 2012 Technology Fast 500, based on its extraordinary five-year revenue growth of 4,412 percent.
- We were ranked as the fifth fastest-growing tech company in New York.
- I was nominated as Entrepreneur of the Year by Ernst & Young.
- Massive press coverage surrounded us, including my personal appearances on CNBC, Bloomberg News, and other major media outlets.
- Wall Street had taken notice of SNAP Interactive with favorable stock analyst reports.
- Hall of Fame entrepreneurs like Mark Cuban, Tim Ferriss, and Gary Vaynerchuk were contacting me for business relationships.
- We were recognized as viral experts on Facebook, (they even highlighted us as a case-study).
- We raised $8.5 million in capital from institutional investors, valuing us at nearly $100 million.
- From 2007 to 2011, our stock price grew more than 1,000 percent.

All the things we set out to accomplish were happening, including gaining recognition and achieving explosive growth. With all those successes swirling around us, the possibility of our grand ambitions growing even more massively became reality.

SPENDING SPREE

The first thing most companies do when they raise a lot of money—like we did in 2011—is to start spending it. We needed to reinvest that capital to grow further. Otherwise, why bother raising the money at all? We also needed to justify the high price of our stock value; it wasn't going to stay that high if we didn't. One way to do that was to make sure the revenue kept growing. Therefore, we did what most companies in our position would have done, which was to spend a lot of money on user acquisition. Fortunately, superior real-time analytics had become part of our business model, so we didn't buy users recklessly.

Next on the list was to get some "adults in the room." SNAP Interactive was a collection of twentysomethings, led by an elder statesman of thirty-two. Investors and analysts kept stating that we needed a much more "experienced" management team as a public company. So, in a move to gain more respect and recognition on Wall Street, we hired very aggressively.

We listened to what the "experts" on Wall Street said, and we grew our staff from a collection of young "must-haves" to an expanded talent pool with a lot of more "experienced" people making over $200,000 per year. Those people looked great on paper, were impressive to outsiders, and gave us a nice bump in perceived maturity as an organization, but unfortunately, they were a total culture clash. To some of the younger people in the office with their sleeves rolled up, a lot of the new hires probably looked like high-priced Wall Street window dressing. Ironically, we were in such an emerging and developing industry that the people with useful "experience" were generally also in their twenties.

As an inexperienced CEO at the time, I knew the increase in personnel from twelve to nearly fifty employees in just a year would introduce new challenges, but I greatly underestimated its impact.

One giant issue was our development cycle. We were a very lean and agile organization. We wanted to start the morning with an idea, build it, and push it live to users the next day. We would often perform twenty to thirty code pushes in a single day. That became a big problem, however, when we hired high-priced senior leaders who were used to pushing one new feature per month (or quarter), because they wanted to thoroughly test, measure, and perfect each feature before launch. In reality, all that did was massively slow down our ability to learn quickly and iterate—our bread and butter—which slowed our innovation greatly.

The old saying goes, "Perfect is the enemy of good," and we lived by those words at SNAP Interactive. We knew it wasn't in our best interest to build perfect features, but to push new features out fast, because our users expected a steady dose of new and interesting ideas to keep them coming back. The more features and optimizations we released, the more we could test. The more we could test, the more we learned about our users, which rapidly expanded our business intelligence and subsequently, our ability to develop a superior product. Our credo was to learn fast and fail fast, if need be—but that's not the world our new hires had lived in.

"The only way to win is to learn faster than anyone else."

—ERIC RIES, AUTHOR OF *THE LEAN STARTUP: HOW TODAY'S ENTREPRENEURS USE CONTINUOUS INNOVATION TO CREATE RADICALLY SUCCESSFUL BUSINESSES*

FAILING ORGANIZATIONAL HEALTH

Almost overnight, our burn rate—how much money we spent compared to how much money came in—went through the roof, due to the payroll required to keep the high-priced (but not so compatible) talent onboard. We became so singularly focused on increasing revenue to appease Wall Street and their enormous growth expectations that we lost sight of the ball. Explosive growth was still occurring, but profitability and corporate culture were suffering. Our overall organizational health was failing.

One lesson I learned too late when trying to solve the culture clash was if there's an employee who looks good on paper, but doesn't reflect the company's values, I should let them go sooner rather than later. Sometimes an employee just isn't a good fit, even if they have a plethora of institutional knowledge, an impressive acumen of valuable experience, and other qualities that seem invaluable. I recommend asking, "Would I hire this person again, knowing what I know now?" Almost every time I was in a situation like that, my answer was, "No." It's extremely counterproductive to continue throwing good time and money at bad resources. The longer that person is kept at a position that everybody knows isn't working out, the worse it is for both parties So, pull the trigger, let the person go, and get on with business. Although firing people is unpleasant, sometimes it's better for both parties to clear the air and get it out of the way quickly.

#ExplosiveGrowthTip 40: Don't hire someone you

wouldn't want to have a beer with after work. Do you want to enjoy a beer with most of your coworkers?

#ExplosiveGrowthTip 41: The threshold question when evaluating a current employee is: would you hire that person again if you could do it over? If not, let them go. Are you in the process of letting employees go who don't pass the "re-hire" test?

Our stock price continued to stay strong until February of that year. At that time, our wayward focus and steadily weakening corporate culture began to affect us, making us dumb all over again.

All the problems that come with being a publicly traded company surfaced one more time. As soon as our stock declined, the massive expectations that were unfulfilled took effect and became a problem.

There was one week in February where the stock went down substantially for no reason that anyone around us could understand. Perhaps the only reason was that if a stock goes up for twenty straight days, it has to come back down at some point. At the same time, it seemed like a new Facebook dating app was coming out every other day. They all attacked the market with one or two new concepts to raise money. The questions and comments about my decision making flooded my phone lines and email inbox.

- 💣 "Did you see this new app?"
- 💣 "Are they going to be better than you?"
- 💣 "Shouldn't you be copying some of the things they're doing?"
- 💣 "Your stock is going way down."
- 💣 "Clearly, you don't know what you're doing anymore."

THE PARTY OF THE YEAR: "ONLY IN THE ALLEY"

Compounding our problems was the never-ending frustration of still not getting our due in Silicon Valley. We also needed to gain deeper connections within the NYC tech scene—dubbed "Silicon Alley." So, I collaborated with my good friend and fellow entrepreneur Chris Mirabile to devise a plan that would address both concerns in grand fashion.

Our idea was to bring together the most interesting and up-and-coming entrepreneurs in NYC, put them in a calendar, and hand-deliver it—along with a party invite—to all the Silicon Valley big-wigs including Mark Zuckerberg. We called the calendar "Only in the Alley" as a way to say Silicon Alley had arrived.

We were able to create an epic event and calendar with

contributions from Mayor Bloomberg's office and its chief digital officer. Mashable's Editor-in-Chief, Adam Ostrow was quoted as saying that it "marks the culmination of a big year in development for New York's broader tech scene." We sent around a hundred invitations to the calendar unveiling party, but word quickly spread. Over 500 people showed up, and eventually we had to shut the doors.

Chris and I targeted NYC-based companies with incredibly smart and passionate founders. It's fascinating to see how successful these companies have been five years later. Several of them became worth hundreds of millions of dollars and potentially more. The entire calendar is located here: http://www.explosive-growth.com/only-in-the-alley-calendar. The participating companies included:

- 💣 **Birchbox** (raised $86+ million)—Hayley Barna and Katia Beauchamp
- 💣 **ClassPass** (originally Classtivity, raised over $150 million)—Payal Kadakia and Sanjiv Sanghavi
- 💣 **ConsumerBell**—Ellie Cachette
- 💣 **Hotlist**—Chris Mirabile and Gianni Martire
- 💣 **Learnvest** (acquired by Northwestern Mutual Life)—Alexa von Tobel
- 💣 **Livestream** (raised $14+ million)—Max Haot, Phil Worthington, Mark Kornfilt, and Dayananda Nanjundappa

- **Plum Benefits** (acquired by Entertainment Benefits Group - EBG)—Shara Mendelson
- **SNAP Interactive** (merged with Paltalk)—Clifford Lerner and Darrell Lerner
- **Thrillist** (raised $50+ million)—Ben Lerer and Adam Rich
- **Xtify** (sold to IBM)—Andrew Weinreich and Josh Rochlin
- **Yipit** (raised $7+ million)—Jim Moran and Vinny Vacanti
- **Zocdoc** (raised $220+ million)—Cyrus Massoumi, Nick Ganju, and Oliver Kharraz, MD

THE *ONLY* THREE METRICS THAT REALLY MATTER

To come up with a solution to our failing organizational health and sustain growth, we asked ourselves, "Why did business start to slow down?" Our obsession with growing revenues at all costs was causing some other key metrics to suffer, while the revenue growth itself was slowing down as well. At that point, we were very data driven, so collecting and analyzing pertinent data seemed like the best approach to begin solving our problem of diminishing growth.

We were measuring and trying to optimize thousands of

metrics, which inadvertently caused us to lose focus on the reasons we were successful—having a remarkable and unique product that users loved to interact with and talk about. We needed to get back to the basics and figure out where we stood with them to understand how to create a new growth rocket. The three critical questions we needed to answer were:

- Was our product still remarkable?
- Did people *love* our product so much that they were telling others about it?
- Were users coming back over and over to use the product?

It's easy for companies big and small to get lost in all the data and lose focus on these three key questions. These three insights are crucial, because they are actionable and predictive of future success, provide invaluable insights with only a handful of users, and are relevant at any stage of your product life cycle.

However, if the product isn't unique, and people don't love it (and don't keep using it), at some point, you will start failing and it may be difficult to comprehend the reason. On the other hand, if these three questions can be answered with favorable results, all the other metrics will fall in line, and success is imminent.

Fortunately, it was pretty easy to measure these things and get the relevant answers we needed.

The three questions above correlate to the only three metrics that really matter:

- 💣 Whether or not a Unique Selling Proposition exists (USP)
- 💣 What the Net Promoter Score is (NPS)
- 💣 User Retention

Obviously, there are numerous other metrics you'll need to measure in order to manage and grow your business including growth, engagement, and profitability metrics. The problem with most of them is they do little to tell you *why* your product is underperforming. The reason USP, NPS, and retention are the only ones that *really* matter is that they tell you *why* your product is underperforming, and hopefully give you the insight you'll need to fix it.

For example, let's say you look at poor growth or profitability metrics alone, and start firing underperforming employees. Then you begin thinking about new ways to grow and creating different marketing ideas. However, this will likely be a fruitless exercise, because the problem is most likely that your product simply sucks, and no amount of growth hacks, new talent, or new marketing tactics will overcome that. Whereas, if your NPS isn't good (meaning nobody wants to tell their friends about your product), then the answer is clear: your product sucks! The mystery is solved. Unfortunately, in that case, you have a lot of work to do to fix things, but at least you know where the problem is.

METRIC #1: UNIQUE SELLING PROPOSITION (USP)

Is the product remarkable? When AYI was new on Facebook, there were several remarkable things about it, such as seeing which user's friends liked them, and near-instant signup and profile creation. Now, we had to determine if we were still remarkable enough to stand out from the competition, and regain that elusive and extremely valuable word-of-mouth growth. To measure this, we decided to conduct a simple survey.

Part of the survey included a key customer satisfaction indicator known as the net promoter score (NPS), which the next section covers in more detail. Also within that survey, we included some other key questions related to the overall quality and uniqueness of the customer experience, such as:

- Which features of AreYouInterested? do you use?
- What is your biggest frustration with AreYouInterested?

- 💣 What would make you more likely to tell your friends about AreYouInterested?
- 💣 Do you have any suggestions to make AreYouInterested? better?
- 💣 What is the one sentence that best describes AreYouInterested?

That last question was crucial, because it told us if the majority of our users were experiencing something magical about the product. Users must come away with a singular message they'll share with friends, otherwise, the message will never stick and spread. For example, Amazon's original unique offering was to offer any book cheaper than the competition, and it worked beyond perfection.

We needed to know not only if our product was unique and had a great customer experience, but also if our branding was working.

Although there is no hard and fast rule about what comprises a good metric for it, I'd argue that a great USP is when at least 50 percent of the users identify the *same* remarkable item that best describes the product in one sentence.

 #ExplosiveGrowthTip 42: Can you describe your product's USP in one concise sentence? Is it truly remarkable?

#ExplosiveGrowthTip 43: Have you asked your users to describe your product in one sentence? Did at least half of the responses refer to the same concept?

Book Recommendation: *Made to Stick: Why Some Ideas Survive and Others Die*, by Chip Heath.

The results of that one question were eye-opening. We got answers that were all over the map, which meant we didn't have one magical thing—a truly unique selling proposition—that customers fell in love with. That result meant either everything was remarkable to some users, or very little was remarkable to others. In our case, it was clearly the latter. This explained why our growth, especially organic growth, was stalling.

AYI was no longer remarkable. We would have to go back to the drawing board, because I didn't see long-term success without regaining the ability to grow organically. The cost of acquiring users on Facebook was increasing by the day, because hundreds of millions of dollars had been raised by other companies—some much bigger than ours—that were building Facebook apps.

As a result, we spent a full year innovating to rebuild and relaunch as a "social discovery site" where users would meet new people through mutual friends and interests.

Rebranding with Similar Interests

We believed we had the largest collection of user interests in the industry. Because our users' profiles were linked to their Facebook profiles, we had an average of over seventy-eight different interests per profile. Our idea was to leverage that data to create an extraordinary experience of matching users based on similar interests. For example, a user who indicated they liked 90s sitcoms would be matched with someone who indicated they liked *Seinfeld* or *Friends*.

Unfortunately, this required categorizing tens of thousands of interests, because all the Facebook interests weren't structured. For example, an interest like *Seinfeld* wasn't associated with any other attributes, such as 90s sitcoms. We wanted to create a proprietary matching system based on similar interests, which was something singles identified as the most important thing in a successful relationship. We also believed this had potential because we would then integrate that system into other sites such as StubHub, and offer discounted date experiences based on similar interests. For example, if two users both liked 80s music, we could offer 10 percent off Billy Joel tickets for his upcoming nearby concert.

Friends of Friends of Friends

By now, most of our competitors had also integrated the

concept of mutual friends, because Facebook made that very easy. It was an enormously popular feature, and we thought we could make it even better by expanding it to friends of friends of friends. Unfortunately, Facebook didn't provide this sort of information, so we had to build the feature ourselves.

Because it was truly a "big data" undertaking, using technologies unfamiliar to our company, I envisioned having the bulk of my team working on this feature for months. However, an unproven (but ambitious) engineer named David Fox boldly said he would take the lead on the task and deliver results. Having already witnessed his passion for his craft, and learning from past experiences, I gave him the chance to build something that would sing.

Ultimately, my faith in him was rewarded, because in just weeks, he almost single-handedly built something that matched up billions of social connections. Once again, the power of a terrific engineer—A-list talent—led to extraordinary results.

"Someone who is exceptional in their role is not just a little better than someone who is pretty good...they are 100 times better."
—MARK ZUCKERBERG, COFOUNDER OF
FACEBOOK AND INTERNET ENTREPRENEUR

The relaunch was a sizable undertaking for our organization. We became the first company to introduce the "friends of friends" concept in online dating. A user could meet new people through mutual friends and friends of friends of friends, or, in Facebook terms, meet singles through a user's social graph. Just knowing users had a friend in common—even if it was a second-degree relationship—was important to singles, especially women.

Through this relaunch, we had created a powerful new way to connect people, something nobody else was doing. It looked like a great feature, so we ran the same survey asking the same question once again a few months after launch: "What is the one sentence that best describes AreYouInterested?" The numbers didn't budge—people still didn't have a salient conception of our product.

You Don't Get a Second Chance to Make a First Impression

We learned a very painful but valuable lesson from that survey: it's very difficult to change what a product is in the eyes of the existing user.

We implemented a bunch of new features that definitely added to the user experience, but nobody recognized that. Even more frustrating, several other new dating sites were getting very popular and growing rapidly with the same features.

A product named Hinge used the same concept of meeting people through mutual friends, and it gained great notoriety for it. It became the core of their brand, because they arrived on the online dating space with it. That feature wasn't associated with our brand, because people already identified us with their first impression of us. We were the Facebook dating app—the original—and that's how people were going to think of us, no matter what we did with AYI going forward.

The other thing that hurt us was we had become a paid app, and those new apps were all free. At that point, Facebook users weren't paying for apps or content within apps. All those new features we added were great, but they didn't do anything to change our brand, solve our problems, or improve our bottom line. Sadly, the most eye-opening result of that survey came from answers to the crucial survey question: What is the one sentence that best describes AYI? Most users said we were the Facebook dating app that costs money.

It didn't help that start-ups were raising tens of millions of dollars in funding, and a new competitor was offering a free product seemingly every day. Our biggest problem was like it or not (not), our "paid" business model had become our identity.

METRIC #2: NET PROMOTER SCORE

The NPS is an underutilized yet incredibly effective way to measure customer satisfaction. Our survey asked how likely users were to recommend our product to a friend or colleague on a scale from zero to ten. The responses were evaluated as follows:

- A response of nine or ten means a user is a "raving promoter of your product."
- A response of seven or eight means a user is a "passive promoter of your product."
- Any rating from zero to six means a user is a detractor.

WHY BE SO HARD ON YOURSELF?

On the surface, it may seem a bit unreasonable to require a rating of seven or above for a user to be considered a promoter. However, the survey was trying to establish the potential for users to "actively promote" our product. If someone rated our product a six, they likely thought it was a decent product—above average—but they weren't likely to rave about it to friends. On the lower end of the scale, it didn't really matter if someone rated the product a zero or a three, because either way, they didn't like it. That person was a detractor, and there wasn't much we could do to change their mind.

On the other hand, if someone rated the product a nine, that meant they thought highly of the product, and were likely to rave about it to their friends and family. It was likely the product was something they wanted to bring up in conversation, because they found it so unique and interesting—definitely magical, a true USP.

 #ExplosiveGrowthTip 44: Ask if users have *already* recommended your product to a friend. Do you know what percentage of your users have recommended your product to a friend? If they said no, try to find out why. Perhaps you just haven't made it easy enough for users to share your product—an easy fix.

To calculate an NPS, simply subtract the percentage of detractors from the percentage of promoters. The NPS score ranges from -100 (everybody is a detractor) to +100 (everybody is a promoter). An NPS above zero (indicating more promoters than detractors) is desirable, but an NPS above fifty is viewed as an extremely positive indicator. Unfortunately for us, we learned that our NPS wasn't very good, which explained why our organic growth had slowed.

The combination of a less-than-stellar NPS with some unfavorable responses to our additional questions was a rude awakening for us, but it also provided clarity as to why certain metrics were performing so poorly. As stated previously, surface metrics won't usually reveal big-picture branding problems, such as the product being boring and ordinary. You may be winning the battle with short-term optimizations, but losing the war with a product that still isn't unique and valuable enough for users to tell their friends about.

The data told us we still needed more innovation to achieve a true USP and a great NPS. We needed to make our product remarkable (again) so users would want to spread the word. The mutual friends concept, and even the second-degree-of-friends idea wasn't going to be enough. We needed to go back to the drawing board at least one more time.

#ExplosiveGrowthTip 45: Are you actively measuring

your NPS? Is your NPS above fifty? Don't waste time and money by trying to market and grow a product that has a poor NPS.

Early-stage companies are obsessively focused on growth, usually at the expense of retention. That methodology is backwards, because retention should be the north-star metric of any early-stage product. If someone builds a great product that users keep coming back to, it will be easy to figure out how to grow it (raise money, spend money on acquiring users, ask users to share it, etc.) However, if a product has a low NPS, and you continue to focus on growing it, that's like saying to the user, "Hey, my product sucks. Want to buy it?"

#ExplosiveGrowthTip 46: Marketing a product with a low NPS is essentially saying to potential customers, "Hey, my product sucks, come check it out."

METRIC #3: RETENTION

Ultimately, retention is the most important metric to measure for any online business—if people keep coming back to the product, every other problem becomes of little significance. Establishing AYI's initial user base was valuable, but we could always pay users to try it. We couldn't, however, pay users to keep coming back, day after day, week after week, and month after month. An understanding of what drove users to continue to use the product repeatedly was the most important insight we had. A strong retention rate is irrefutable data that proves people love your product, and I believe the same goes for most businesses.

What drives people to continuously use an online dating site is a great user experience—that magic moment of getting messages (and ultimately dates) from people they want to meet. Getting a reply to an email from a potentially special someone on an online dating site will keep that user coming back, over and over. Of course, if that reply leads to a serious relationship, then to a commitment, then maybe the dating app did too good of a job; but that's a whole different problem.

FACEBOOK'S MAGIC NUMBER
FOR RETENTION

In the early days of Facebook, the leaders recognized a drastic difference in retention based on how many friends each user had in their first ten days. If a user had less than seven friends, it wasn't interesting to them and they didn't come back to the site often, as their newsfeed just wasn't active enough to keep them engaged. However, if a user had seven or more friends within ten days after signing up, the retention rate was very high, as the newsfeed seemingly came to life. It's probably a much different number now, but seven was their magic number in those days and early Facebook employees implied this was a watershed moment for them.

Another key metric that Facebook was obsessed with was getting 90 percent of its users to login six out of seven days per week. Obviously, any product that gets that kind of retention is going to be wildly successful.

The lesson here is that not only is it crucial to measure retention, but it's also crucial to understand what ultimately drives users to come back to the product—your product's "aha" moment. This can be figured out by separating out the high-retention users from low-retention users and analyzing the data to look for what makes the high-retention users different from others. Do they have more friends (Facebook)? Do they have more replies (AYI)?

That insight alone can change the business, because it explains what to optimize for.

For us, it was obvious to see in the data that high retention users got lots of replies, and users who had few replies didn't bother to come back. With that type of insight, we were able to enhance the experience for the users who were lacking replies, including improving our algorithms to surface better potential matches and building features such as "Priority Placement," where they could pay for increased exposure in order to get more replies, hopefully leading to higher retention.

#ExplosiveGrowthTip 47: Do you know what single user action or experience compels users to come back to your product repeatedly? If not, figure it out now, because this could be the most important insight you need to grow your business.

Once Facebook discovered that "lucky seven" was their goal, they focused serious labor on raising the number of friends on every user's profile. They did this by suggesting friends based on data that nobody else was thinking about. Users logged in and saw friend suggestions based on a fourth-grade classmate, a person their third cousin met at a bar in Albuquerque a few years ago, and other previously unrecognized variables. They immediately become enamored with a connection to a potentially long-lost friend or the excitement of connecting with someone on the outer circle of their life.

The ideal retention metric for any online business should be based on how frequently a user comes back, what percentage of users come back in a certain time frame, or any combination thereof. Generally, one, thirty, ninety, and 360-day data should be sufficient to gauge retention rates, but it's still important to discover *why* users keep coming back.

#ExplosiveGrowthTip 48: Growth without retention is worthless. However, retention without growth is a problem any entrepreneur should love to have, because it means people love the product. Do you know what your one-day and thirty-day retention is?

#ExplosiveGrowthTip 49: Don't spend significant money on marketing until your one-day and thirty-day retention is well above average for your industry.

9

SOLVING PROBLEMS AND SUSTAINING GROWTH THROUGH VISION, VALUES, AND DATA

"Good business leaders create a vision, articulate the vision, passionately own the vision, and relentlessly drive it to completion."

—JACK WELCH, AUTHOR AND CEO OF GE FROM 1981-2001

Finding a solution to our declining organizational health became my number one priority. Through my own experience and by observing other organizations, it became clear to me that a healthy organization could overcome any problems and thrive. At its core, a healthy organization has happy, passionate, and highly motivated employees, all executing with the same clear and concise goals in mind, which will likely translate to success. With that in mind, my approach to repair our organizational health was twofold:

- I brought in expertise to help me and my staff better understand how to scale an organization and how to make it run smoothly.
- I educated myself through intensive and borderline obsessive-compulsive reading of various books on management, leadership, and scaling a larger organization to learn from others' successes and mistakes.

BRING IN THE EXPERTS

They say the best teacher is experience, but since I didn't have time to learn completely on the job, I brought in experience from the outside by hiring an advisory board. This board was staffed with various advisors who had "been there, done that" and their purpose was to advise and mentor me and the team a few times per week.

Not all the experts I hired were consultants. Josh, one of

the best hires we ever made, was brought in to run our product and analytics team. He immediately went to work and implemented a highly effective process improvement strategy called CIO, which stood for Celebrate, Iterate, or Obliterate.

CELEBRATE, ITERATE, OR OBLITERATE (CIO)

CIO was a huge process improvement strategy for us, because we were running so many tests in those days that we began to suffer from data overload. It became very difficult to keep track of all the new ideas and latest builds while analyzing the results. Worse than that, was that the code became bloated, because the engineers had a hard time incorporating all the existing tests, which may or may not have still been around in a few months. The result of that inefficiency was that not only did our metrics suffer, but ironically, our ability to quickly build new features eroded as well.

The CIO concept put a simple process in place to follow every time we launched a new feature. Within two weeks after release, we would run tests, analyze the data, and take one of three actions:

- 💣 Celebrate it!: It was a huge win and surpassed our success metric!

- 💣 Iterate on it: We thought it had potential, but it didn't quite live up to expectations yet.
- 💣 Obliterate it: It was a complete disaster and wasn't worth our time to iterate it.

That simple process forced us to remove a lot of features that weren't adding enough to the user experience or didn't work out for some other reason. This alone was a huge success as bombarding the site with new features not only slowed down the development time of each successive feature, but also diminished the user experience. We learned that sometimes users didn't know what to do with all the shiny, new objects.

Much to my surprise, product managers and engineers got more excited when we obliterated a feature than when we celebrated a win, because it meant less code for them to manage, and it made it easier to build new things. Meanwhile, I developed my own reasons for becoming excited about obliterations—we saw incremental improvements in usage as we decluttered the site by removing rarely used features.

 #ExplosiveGrowthTip 50: Do you have any features that are rarely used? If so, do you have a plan to obliterate them in the next thirty days?

#ExplosiveGrowthTip 51: Do you have a process to actively evaluate new features? If not, implement CIO (Celebrate, Iterate, Obliterate) ASAP.

EXTRA! EXTRA! READ ALL ABOUT IT

The second thing I did to repair our organizational health was to inhale every book I could find on what separates great companies from the good and not-so-good, and how to scale a growing organization. My crazy plan was to read one complete book on leadership every night and implement all the lessons I learned from it the next morning at the office. Strangely enough, many of the lessons I learned this way worked out very favorably for the company.

Some of my favorites were *Good to Great* and *Built to Last,* both by Jim Collins, *Mastering the Rockefeller Habits* by Verne Harnish, and a bunch of books by Patrick Lencioni: *The Advantage: Why Organizational Health Trumps Everything Else in Business, Death by Meeting,* and *Five Dysfunctions of the Team: A Leadership Fable.*

CREATING VISION AND A MISSION

One of the books I read explained how to create a compelling organizational mission and vision. The next morning, I came into the office determined to put the words from that book into action. I don't remember exactly which book it was (because I read so many of them), but it said that our mission needs to "inspire people, last many years, and provide clear guidelines about what ideas the company would pursue, while giving people the freedom to contribute without micromanaging all decisions from the top down."

That morning, I proclaimed to my staff, "Okay, our corporate vision isn't clear enough. We are going to focus our efforts on creating a compelling vision for the entire organization to be a part of."

I went on, "Here's Google's: 'Organize the world's information and make it universally accessible and useful.' Here's Facebook's: 'Give people the power to share and make the world more open and connected.' Those are just examples, but we need something like that."

A few days later, we had a mission: "Eliminate Loneliness."

We further described it as: "We build innovative solutions to make it fun and easy to meet new people in order to enrich people's lives."

I later learned it was actually Mike Sherov's wife, Marissa, who came up with the whole concept. Mike's brilliance was in full force in that moment. Realizing that a bunch of twenty-year-old internet nerds were not ideally qualified to come up with a mission for an online dating company, he called upon his wife for inspiration.

Creating this mission statement was very impactful and inspirational. It gave a lot of people a great reason to come to work every day. They felt like they were part of something greater than merely trying to improve marketing ROIs and getting more users. Plus, it didn't mean we had to exclusively focus on online dating, as it was becoming increasingly clear that a lot of people also used dating sites just to make new friends, which was a much larger opportunity. That mission influenced every decision we made thereafter, and proved to be incredibly inspirational to all, while providing the focus we needed in pursuing new ideas. I knew our mission was having an impact when I overheard somebody at a karaoke outing ask Mike what his job was at SNAP, and he replied, "I bang on the keyboard and babies are made."

 #ExplosiveGrowthTip 52: Do you have a concise and inspiring vision and mission statement?

CORE VALUES

Why did we hire some people who weren't a great fit for

our corporate culture? One of the books I read suggested that it was because we didn't have a clear set of corporate values that would define the type of people who would thrive within our culture. With that idea fresh in my mind, another one of my mandates was to come up with five core values for the organization to run by. Here's what we came up with:

1. **Experiment.** We use a scientific, data-driven method to make decisions. We hypothesize, experiment, learn, and iterate. We find innovative solutions and question assumptions, even if they are longstanding. Experimentation and iterative steps guide even our most innovative ideas.

2. **Own It.** Our passion comes through in how we work. If we see something that needs to be fixed, we take the initiative to not only fix it, but to do it well. Then, we hunt down the next opportunity for improvement and make it happen. This applies not only to our work but also to ourselves. We actively pursue self-improvement and make ourselves experts in our fields, whether it's by taking classes, reading forums, or joining book clubs.

3. **Be Quick.** Signed, sealed and delivered! We do things quickly and in MVP form. We have a bias for action and speed over perfection. We prefer an ugly but accurate report today over a fancily formatted

report tomorrow. The faster we move, the faster we fail, and the faster we learn. To help us move quickly, we automate wherever possible.

4. **Plan and Execute.** A goal without a plan is just a wish. We commit to lean plans and processes, and then we follow through on them to get results. We remain nimble. If we realize we're heading in the wrong direction, we're quick to embrace change, make a new plan, and get on a new course.

5. **Collaborate.** Great ideas can come from anyone, so we create a safe and open environment in which we're always exchanging ideas. For collaboration to work, hearing is as essential as being heard. That's why we seek first to understand and then to be understood. When we hit a bump in the road, we focus on learning, not on blaming. Since we value each other's ideas, we are able to spar intellectually one moment and then grab beers together in the next.

We put posters up all over the office to remind everyone of what the organization stood for (Note: We discovered that the bathroom was the most effective location for the posters to get people's attention). That list of core values served as continuing motivation, because everyone could feel like they were part of this unique value system, and they all understood their role in carrying out those items. Furthermore, to reinforce our values in practice, we encouraged employees to praise others who excelled at one of our core values. At our weekly all-hands meetings, we'd reward those employees and give them a prize.

More importantly, the core values helped us scale the organization, because as we were growing, they empowered people to make decisions on their own. Otherwise, the leader makes all the decisions, forming a virtual tyranny, which I wanted no part of and neither did anybody else. But, if I was the only one who knew what our values were, then I would have been the only one truly capable of making decisions. Conversely, if the employees felt empowered to accept responsibility for quality and take ownership of the product, they were going to have a few things to say about how decisions were made.

Ultimately, identifying our five core values also allowed us to identify potential new hires who would be a good fit for our organization. If the values of a candidate didn't align well with ours, we simply moved on to different candidates. For example, we would frequently interview candidates who said they preferred working from home to eliminate distractions (among other reasons). Although this makes sense in certain organizations, our core value of collaboration meant it didn't work for ours, and it made it easy to eliminate such candidates.

A great quick way to identify core values is to look within the organization and identify people who represent the ideal employee. After that, it should be easy to discover what qualities make those employees special, and be able to identify related core values from that discovery process.

 #ExplosiveGrowthTip 53: Do you have documented core values? Does every employee know them? Are you doing anything to actively reinforce them?

TEN AWESOME OFFICE CULTURE HACKS

As cofounder of the company, my brother Darrell made office culture one of his primary areas of focus. Largely inspired by his hard work and determination, we were eventually able to cure our cultural ills, and even had a very complimentary piece written about us in *Business Insider* titled, "Why Gamers Love Working for Facebook Dating-App Developer SNAP Interactive."

The key to this healthy turnaround for us was a series of creative "office culture hacks" we implemented to make everyone look forward to coming to work on Mondays. Darrell even featured them in a popular blog post later on.

Looking back, there were probably over 100 different things we did to turn our company culture into one worth bragging about, but I thought I'd call out a few of the highlights. What's worth noting is that these are primarily small things that any company can introduce into their own office environment to instantly improve their office culture.

1. **Massage Day.** This is a big winner—trust me, and it's not nearly as expensive as it sounds. We simply hired someone to come in for a few hours every week or every other week, and we offered fifteen-minute chair massages to all employees. It takes very little time away from work and it isn't very costly, but it's something employees really look forward to. Plus, it's a really cool perk to be able to advertise in your recruiting package.

2. **Company Newsletter.** As we grew in size, it became more difficult for employees to learn about each other on a personal basis. So, we began a quarterly newsletter where we'd include everything from company highlights and event pictures to employee birthdays and milestones, as well as profiles and interviews with new employees.

3. **Summer Fridays.** From Memorial Day to Labor Day, we'd allow employees to leave any time after 4:00 p.m. on Fridays. The couple of hours in lost productivity were more than made up for by the goodwill generated. We even encouraged employees to submit photos of

how they were spending their Summer Friday, and we put a collage of them into the newsletter.

4. **Birthday Donations.** As we grew, it became difficult to acknowledge birthdays on an individual basis, and it was also challenging to find a convenient time to gather everyone together for cake. Still, we wanted to continue celebrating employee birthdays, so we came up with the cool idea of offering employees $100 to donate to the charity of their choice on their birthday. Employees were asked to write a paragraph explaining what the charity was, who it helped, and why they selected it. Then we'd include each of these write-ups in the company newsletters for all to read. This is a simple "feel good" item that simultaneously helps good causes.

5. **Timeline.** We recreated the "History of SNAP" in a timeline that went across the entirety of one of our whiteboard walls. The timeline contained a picture of each employee right above their start date along with key company milestones.

6. **Ping-Pong.** Everyone loves ping-pong, but I never imagined what a hit this would be in the office. Employees would retreat to the ping-pong table for a quick game during the day and specifically stay late just to get in a few more matches. We even began holding tournaments to determine the office champ (the entire company would gather round to watch the

finals), and I went so far as to order a custom-made WWF-style championship belt to award to the winner. A little friendly competition goes a long way toward team bonding.

7. **Chipwich Wednesday.** Every Wednesday afternoon, we'd all take a short break to gather in the conference room and enjoy a tasty dessert. On a rotating basis, each employee would get the chance to select a treat for the entire office. We'd give them a budget of around fifty dollars, and employees would have fun trying to one-up each other in coming up with something creative. Some desserts were homemade while others were purchased (by those less inclined to bake), but they were all great. Named for the first office dessert ever purchased, Chipwich Wednesday was always a weekly hit.

8. **A Warm Welcome for New Employees.** They say first impressions mean everything, so we wanted to make sure new employees went home smiling (rather than stressing) on their first day. We'd have funny balloons waiting for them at their desk, give them a small bottle of our custom-labeled champagne to celebrate their arrival, and introduce them to a "buddy" whose job it was to take them out to lunch on their first day (and answer any questions they might have).

9. **The Culture Club.** I put together a group of some of the most creative and enthusiastic employees specif-

ically for the purpose of working on culture-related activities. We'd meet regularly, and new and creative activities (like the ones on this list) would emerge every time. We called ourselves the "Culture Club," and yes, some meetings even included the playing of "Karma Chameleon!"

10. **"Excuse Me, I Believe You Have My [Anniversary] Stapler.**" With so much focus on recruiting new employees in the start-up world, we thought it would be nice to acknowledge those who stay with us for a while. We came up with the hilarious idea to mark an employee's one-year anniversary at SNAP by awarding them a red Swingline stapler, engraved with their name. We presented it to them at the company-wide morning meeting on their one-year anniversary. People loved this, and new employees would eagerly count down the days until they earned their stapler and could post a picture of it on Facebook.

Changing an office culture requires time, effort, and a commitment to the cause, but I learned that little things go a long way. We spend more time with the people we work with than we do with our families, so making the workplace fun and bringing employees closer together pays dividends in spades.

 #ExplosiveGrowthTip 54: Do you offer fifteen-minute

in-office massages to all employees at least monthly? Trust me, do it.

THE NINETY-DAY SPRINT: A 400 PERCENT INCREASE IN REPLIES!

"If you could get all the people in an organization rowing in the same direction, you could dominate any industry, in any market, against any competition, at any time."

—PATRICK LENCIONI, AUTHOR OF ELEVEN BUSINESS BOOKS INCLUDING, *THE FIVE DYSFUNCTIONS OF A TEAM: A LEADERSHIP FABLE.*

If I could pick the one event that went the furthest in helping us to get healthy again, it was the ninety-day sprint.

In the book, *Built to Last: Successful Habits of Visionary Companies*, the authors (Jim Collins and Jerry Porras) discuss the concept of a BHAG (Big Hairy Audacious Goal) as a way to drive continuous innovation. They argue that the right BHAG is so motivational that the whole organization becomes obsessed with it, and it galvanizes the company. It should be noted that Collins's idea of a BHAG was more along the lines of President Kennedy declaring that a man would land on the moon by the end of the decade. Though our goals at SNAP were considerably less ambitious, I still became intrigued by that notion. I thought a BHAG was a good way for everyone to feel like they contributed to the most important goal of the company, while also not being distracted by so many goals and priorities.

If everyone knows about and shares a common focus, each decision made by each employee is likely to be made with that overarching goal or objective in mind. That should result in all of the company's other Key Performance Indicators (KPIs) or goals increasing as well, because of a trickle-down effect to productivity.

In his book, *The 8th Habit, From Effectiveness To Greatness,* Stephen Covey compares an organization with different goals to a wildly dysfunctional soccer team. This sports analogy resonated strongly with me, as I thought of my experience as the team captain of my high school basketball team.

I remembered how magical it was when everyone on the team knew the plays and was working together. It seemed like we could take on the version of Team USA that had Magic, Michael, and Larry on it (sure, we could). However, if just one of us went rogue, it was challenging at best to get anything done. If one person was more focused on padding his scoring rather than winning, we could lose to anybody, even the 2016 Brooklyn Nets (although, I like our chances regardless of any ball-hog in that one).

Based on that profound interpretation of the facts, I surveyed my employees to discover what they believed our highest priorities and goals were, expecting everybody to know the answer. However, the answers were all over the map—another wake-up call for me. But the results also got me excited, because I was ready to make drastic changes, and the sports analogy really hit home for me. I just needed to make it crystal clear what the goal was and how we were going to get there. After all, if we could get that far without a uniform goal, imagine what would happen when we were all properly aligned.

Our numbers were declining at that point, and I knew we needed to make some changes. We had approximately twenty different goals and KPIs. I knew we needed to pick just one that would get our organizational engine revving again.

I literally took pages from some of the books I was reading, made copies, and handed them out to everyone in the office. I told them we should figure out the one thing we needed to achieve as an organization more than anything else.

As I've said before, the most magical experience a user

can have on an online dating site is a reply to their message, because it means the person they are interested in is interested in them as well. From that observation, we determined that increasing the replies to a user's initial message on our site was going to be our organizational focus, our BHAG. Ultimately, the goal was to increase revenues, but we needed a more tangible and narrowly focused goal that we could directly affect. We ran some basic correlation analyses, and realized that users getting replies to their messages directly correlates very strongly to revenue. That wasn't surprising, as the more replies a user received, the more they came back to the site, and the more they paid us. At the time, AYI was getting around 80,000 replies each day, and our unified ninety-day goal was to double that figure.

That was a lofty goal, because that number of replies had been relatively stable for a year. However, I truly believe small goals equal small ideas. I always encourage (and sometimes insist upon) very aggressive goals, because the ideas and thought processes always seem to lead to far better ideas and ultimately better outcomes. Some employees love this and some don't, which again comes down to the core values.

We would forego discussing all other KPIs during the ninety-day period, and focus exclusively on doubling our replies. Furthermore, we would do it by getting the entire company involved. The staff was broken up into teams, and each team got to try their ideas on 10 percent of the site's audience. The team that had the best results would win prizes.

#Explosive Growth Tip 55: Are most of your employees working on something to help the company reach a single critical goal?

What Motivates Me, May Not Motivate You

When a goal or objective is important enough, I learned that it makes sense to use highly motivational tactics.

My Wall Street background led me to believe that everyone was motivated by money, but it turns out that's not really true.

As a businessman, I was motivated by creating a great product, which would translate into more profits and ultimately a higher stock price. However, I soon learned that others did not share those same motivations, and this was especially true of engineers. For example, some engineers said that working on new and complicated challenges and technologies was the most motivating factor for them in their jobs. Others said that working on something that impacted millions was their biggest motivation. Hardly any of them—even when pressed—said compensation was the most important motivator for them.

I learned that different things motivated different people. Note that even though most people could afford the cash equivalent of the prize I offered, something non-monetary still usually motivated them much better than money, because it might be something they enjoyed, but wouldn't necessarily buy on their own. Once I figured that out, I spent a lot of time and put tremendous effort into giving out some really special prizes.

#ExplosiveGrowthTip 56: Figure out what motivates every employee, and understand that their motivations may be different than yours. Are you asking each interviewee and employee what would make them more excited about coming to work every day?

After asking everyone in the office what prize would motivate them the most, I settled on the following package: two tickets to the insanely popular Broadway show, *The Book of Mormon*, a steak dinner at any steak house of their choice, a $2,000 Apple gift card, a $5,000 budget to plan a party for their team or the company, and car service to and from work for a week.

Interestingly enough, I learned a valuable lesson on motivating people a little while before the ninety-day sprint that I was able to apply. It was while we were raising money and trying to build a winning corporate culture.

Our office was right next to Madison Square Garden, and I happened to be a huge basketball fan. Not understanding yet that just because something motivated me, didn't mean it motivated someone else. I thought, "Wouldn't it be great to acquire season tickets to the Knicks? What a great recruiting tool!" My plan was to let each employee pick a game, and I was incredibly excited to tell everyone about it.

Much to my surprise, a lot of the women in the office wanted to go to a game (probably just for a night out more than basketball fandom), but almost none of the guys even thought about it, which blew me away.

One of my employees asked me, "How long are the games?"

I said, "They're about two-and-a-half hours—it's the Knicks—you know, the professional basketball team?"

He responded with, "What do I wear?"

I said, "What do you mean, what do you wear? How about pants and a shirt?"

He said, "I mean, do I need to wear a suit or a tuxedo, or anything like that? They're not going to ask me to play, are they?"

That last question really drove the point home—he had no idea about professional basketball, and this incentive was not motivational to him in the least. (Funny postscript to this story: that employee eventually went to a game, and became a huge Knicks fan afterward.)

With proper motivation in mind, everyone split into their teams and worked on coming up with ideas to double replies. The only stipulation in the beginning was that I (along with a couple of other senior leaders) had to approve each idea. We also held a meeting every week to check in on how everyone was progressing in their teams. For ninety days, it was all we focused on. Concerns about revenue and subscriptions were cast aside like an older brother at the homecoming of a new baby.

Of course, what happens when you provide a really awesome prize package as motivation for achieving a goal? Human nature dictates that inevitably, someone will try to find the loophole, or just plain ol' cheat.

People who hadn't contributed an idea for five years all of a sudden got motivated to participate, and that's when we discovered that some proposed ideas were a little too "creative." One such idea was to have a button that would send a user's message to every user on the site. This idea, although crafty, would have been the equivalent of a "Send to All" feature for AYI. This would have technically led to doubling the replies (since every user would be getting inundated with messages), but it would have absolutely demolished the user experience. I obviously had to disqualify that one.

The person who came up with that idea had never contributed any ideas for many years previous to that. After defusing his idea bomb that would have destroyed the site, I asked him if he had any other ideas. Sure enough, he had a few others that were actually very good, and not overly destructive. I probed a little further, asking him, "Where did all this creativity come from?" He said, "I really just wanted to see *The Book of Mormon*." This was proof positive that different people are motivated by different things.

Every team had at least one great idea during the sprint. One of them was to show the user an "unread message" pop-up when they first logged into the site. It was so simple, yet brilliant, that it almost doubled the amount of replies on its own.

Although pop-ups are generally viewed as annoying and thus bad for the user experience, I approved this feature because getting a message was a beautiful experience on the site, so I thought emphasizing it would likely be appreciated by the users. As was usually the case, the data provided some surprising, but great insight. The data showed that the pop-ups were hurting the retention rate for women, because most of them *always* had messages, and constantly getting pop-ups became annoying for them. So, we quickly iterated and made it simple to disable the feature with one click.

Another idea that blew my mind due to its simplistic concept (yet effective result), was to simply increase the number of messages that would appear on the page of the user's in-box. That person said, "It's frustrating to have to click 'next' when I want to see more messages, since we only show ten messages on one page."

Their team initially tried increasing the number of messages on the first page from ten to twenty and achieved a substantial increase in replies. Then they tried thirty, and got an even bigger increase. The next iteration was fifty messages, but at that point, the loading time for the page took too long, and hurt the user experience. We determined that around thirty-five messages was the sweet spot, where the user could see as many messages as possible without loading time becoming a problem.

Most of these ideas came from unexpected places. The best ones didn't come from people with the highest salaries who were normally tasked with generating new ideas. In fact, the largest chunk of them came from the administrative and support staff, who were among the lowest-paid employees at the company. That's another interesting lesson I'm going to take with me wherever I go—seek creativity from everyone in the organization, because you never know where true genius may be hiding. To ensure that I and other leaders remained connected to the users, we had the support team send a weekly summary of the top issues and ideas from users for management to discuss.

Speaking of true genius hiding, one of the ideas was to put a heart icon in the subject line of certain emails. I thought, "That's the dumbest idea I've ever heard." Of course, I didn't say it, because it would have been extremely destructive to the brainstorming process (and to our core values).

The rules of the game indicated that as long as an idea could be reasonably implemented, we had to try it. So, we tested putting a heart icon in the subject line of certain emails, and lo and behold, the amount of emails opened increased by 18 percent.

#ExplosiveGrowthTip 57: Don't be afraid to test any idea,

because you can rarely guess what will and what won't work. Have you tested an idea recently that somebody from your customer service team was passionate about?

What were the results of the ninety-day sprint? Not only did we double replies, but we quintupled them to over 400,000 per day (up from 80,000). This seemingly simple, fun, and interactive company mandate completely reversed the trajectory of the company and helped us grow to $19 million per year in revenue. It contributed greatly to curing our poor organizational health and lack of focus during a time when we desperately needed it.

 #ExplosiveGrowthTip 58: What is the one goal that, if achieved, would solve most other problems? Do you have a plan to obsessively focus on and achieve that one goal?

#ExplosiveGrowthTip 59: Small goals lead to small ideas. Double or triple your goals and use a company-wide brainstorming session to solicit ideas.

Book Recommendation: *The ONE Thing: The Surprisingly Simple Truth Behind Extraordinary Results* by Gary Keller.

HACKATHONS TO THE RESCUE

Another challenge we faced a little later on was that

the overflowing fountain of new users from going viral on Facebook had dried up. We needed to reinvent how we were going to sustain growth. The way we tried to approach most of the challenges we faced was to play to our strengths. We always tried to stay focused, outwork others, and use data to make smart decisions—these were all strengths integral to our success. It didn't take long for us to realize that effective use of data was not only a strength, but could be used effectively to sustain growth.

On the outside, we may have looked like a happy-go-lucky band of techies, whose self-imposed mission was to eliminate loneliness, a novel notion with an altruistic intent for sure. On the inside, however, we were a serious, data-driven, analytical, number-crunching machine. In fact, I realized a little too late that our ability to gather massive amounts of data and quickly analyze it was what separated us from the herd.

We were able to simultaneously run hundreds of experiments that created millions of permutations of our site. Then, we collected the results in real time, and sliced them by any demographic we needed—age, gender, location, and many others to create an optimal experience.

While deep in a several month product roadmap meticulously planned to regain growth, the team started to complain that there was no room for new ideas and inno-vation anymore. That feedback really hit home for me, because I always thought back to the Facebook opportu-nity for us. I knew that such an opportunity would come along again sometime, and I feared we would be too busy with our singular focus to properly notice or pursue it. So, I asked the team for suggestions.

The team suggested we emulate Google, where employees get 20 percent of their time to be creative and work on whatever they want. This concept didn't sit well with me, because it felt too much like playtime.

The next idea was to have hackathons, which was similar in nature, but more structured because everybody had playtime at the same time, and thus could collaborate, which was one of our core values. I still viewed hackathons as a way for people to not work for a full day every week more than anything else, but I was dead wrong.

The monthly hackathons were to be held on the last Friday of the month. To satisfy my concern that it wouldn't be a total waste, we provided a general theme or problem we were trying to solve, in order to give some focus to teams. However, this was just recommended guidance and not a rule, so people could work on anything if they weren't interested in the theme.

Prior to one hackathon, our marketing team said, "I wish there was a way that we could tell how well a campaign would do without waiting several months for the revenue data to come in." A few engineers excitedly took that request as a challenge. They teamed up with the marketing team to see what they could come up with. People who never spoke to each other would team up based on various unmet needs, because they knew certain engineers or data people had a valuable skill set to contribute to a solution.

We built intricate systems via monthly hackathons and hard-working development practices that analyzed millions of data points every minute, and we used them more and more effectively to get press coverage as well.

So, a few people teamed up to try some new ideas and they created something amazing. The new tool could somewhat accurately predict a campaign's long-term ROI based on the user's profile data such as age, gender, city, etc., and the user's initial activity, such as how many people they browsed and how many photos they uploaded. The team proved that the initial user activity could do a solid job of predicting the revenue from that user and campaign for several months onward. This meant we could measure ROI before we even had any revenues from the campaign. What took other companies months was now taking us minutes. As it turned out, we were a big data company that happened to be in the dating business.

#ExplosiveGrowthTip 60: Do your employees have ways to be creative and try their own ideas? Do you have a monthly hackathon?

#ExplosiveGrowthTip 61: Do you have any internally developed tools that may be a better business opportunity on their own than your current product? Are you doing anything to pursue them as a new opportunity?

SURVEY SAYS...

Our users loved finding out various facts and figures about the dating landscape, and so did the media. There's something about human nature that wants to know where we fit in. Most of us are incredibly curious to know what data sets we're a part of, and how much they help or hurt us in attracting others. We realized we had all this data at our fingertips to answer questions that were generally thought of as taboo or controversial, but we found the results so interesting internally that we knew we might have been onto something big.

With Valentine's day approaching, we wanted to get press coverage, because it's the biggest day of the year for singles to get inspired to sign up and pay for a dating site. As usual, we held a company brainstorming session for ideas we could write about, and someone said, "My friend found out she was single when her boyfriend changed his relationship status on Facebook. Are we able to see if that happens a lot on AYI?"

We didn't have the internal data for that particular idea, but a simple survey of our users would give it to us. So, we asked our users if they ever found out their relationship was over by seeing their significant other change their Facebook status. Our survey revealed 25 percent of respondents said, "Yes." In a case like this, misery definitely loves company, so it's possible that when some people are hurting, they just like to see the numbers proving they're not alone. I remember that particular survey got us a lot of press and signups. After those favorable results, we ran with the concept.

I said to everyone, "Okay, that worked out really well for us. Let's come up with some other ideas that could be fun, interesting, or controversial." From that open call for ideas, we got hundreds—maybe thousands—of ideas, and most of them were pretty damned good. This was really the birth of a very important concept for us, which was storytelling using big data. It also led to a widely covered blog we launched called, "The Data of Dating."

Companies spend a lot of money and will do anything to get one story or press release to go viral. Based on our previous success with newsjacking (Britney Spears), along with the Valentine's Day break-up story, it became clear we could use our data or survey our users for content to create a non-stop stream of fun and compelling stories that would grow our brand.

Dozens of the stories ended up going viral with millions of page views and ultimately, significant signups. The playbook for these stories became simple and second nature for us, and could likely be used in many other industries as well. What follows is a concise but comprehensive playbook on "How to Use Storytelling with Big Data:"

1. **Come up with a controversial or interesting topic.** Create a controversial, interesting, or taboo hypothesis that relates to the industry, usually done through a company-wide brainstorm. Example: Do blondes really have more fun?

2. **Crunch the data.** If there isn't enough data or it's just not possible to crunch, survey the users or run a survey using Google Survey to get the necessary results. Example: To calculate if blondes have more fun online, all we needed to do was calculate how often women got liked vs. skipped based on their hair color.

3. **Create a catchy title.** Find the most interesting or

controversial result—something attention-grabbing—
and highlight that in the title. Example: Blondes have
28 percent more fun online.

4. **Create a fun visual.** Create a well-designed visual
   presentation of the data.

5. **Reproduce the story for a different demographic.**
   After the initial story is successful, reproduce the
   same story, but feature a more granular level, such
   as specific location (country, city, state), age range
   (millennials vs. baby boomers) or interest group
   (Android vs. iPhone users) to create numerous viral
   stories around one concept. Example: For the hair
   color story, we broke the results out further by every
   state and then by city, age range, and gender.

The next several subsections include some of our best
and most interesting examples of storytelling with big
data from AYI (which is now called FirstMet). Each of
these stories led to massive media coverage and tens of
thousands of new signups, while keeping our brand front
and center in users' minds. You can find these and other
big data stories online at: http://www.explosive-growth.
com/case-study.

DO BLONDES REALLY HAVE MORE FUN (ONLINE)?

Apparently, they do—at least that's what our research

showed us. Many of the best ideas for data stories came from the women in the company, and doing a data story on hair color was one of the very best they came up with. By analyzing the *like* rates based on women's hair color, we discovered that blonde women get 28 percent more matches than women with other hair colors. That number seemed awfully high to most people who read the article (probably all the non-blondes), but the data was there to back it up.

BALD IS BEAUTIFUL

Although providing data to prove or disprove a commonly held stereotype (such as blondes having more fun) was usually sufficient to generate substantial interest in the story, frequently the data would uncover surprising results, which could add even more value. So, we ran the same hair color data on men, and sure enough, the data revealed that being bald wasn't a detriment at all, because bald men received 5 percent more matches than the average male.

The viral response we got from this story gave us the secret sauce for our recipe for storytelling (the five-step process outlined earlier in this chapter). We went on to leverage this story by adding in several new geographic angles as well.

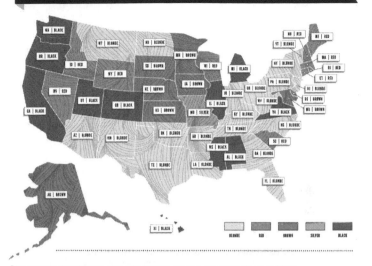

BLONDE   RED   BROWN   SILVER   BLACK

THE BEST CITIES FOR **YOUR HAIR COLOR**

The data below from FirstMet shows which cities like each hair color the most. For example, women with blonde hair get liked the most in Tampa, Florida.

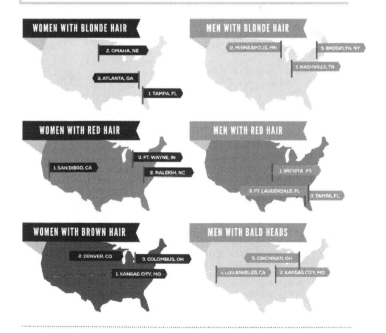

WOMEN WITH BLONDE HAIR
2. OMAHA, NE
3. ATLANTA, GA
1. TAMPA, FL

MEN WITH BLONDE HAIR
2. MINNEAPOLIS, MN
3. BROOKLYN, NY
1. NASHVILLE, TN

WOMEN WITH RED HAIR
1. SAN DIEGO, CA
3. FT. WAYNE, IN
2. RALEIGH, NC

MEN WITH RED HAIR
1. WICHITA, KS
3. FT. LAUDERDALE, FL
2. TAMPA, FL

WOMEN WITH BROWN HAIR
2. DENVER, CO
3. COLOMBUS, OH
1. KANSAS CITY, MO

MEN WITH BALD HEADS
3. CINCINNATI, OH
1. LOS ANGELES, CA
2. KANSAS CITY, MO

ARE YOU ATTRACTING GOLD DIGGERS?

There was a field on the AYI app that allowed the user to select their income range, which is typical of most dating sites. We figured it would be easy to translate the results from that data set to come up with a story that related income to online dating success.

Not surprisingly, each dollar a user earned did increase their attractiveness online. The key takeaway was that men earning more than $150,000 annually received 53 percent more messages than men earning less than $40,000 annually. Overall, the data indicated a 17.8 percent *like* rate for the higher income guys compared to an 11.6 percent *like* rate for the less wealthy.

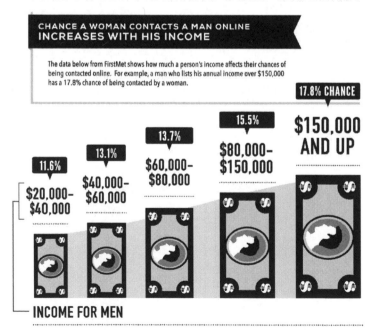

ARE YOU ATTRACTING GOLD-DIGGERS?

CHANCE A WOMAN CONTACTS A MAN ONLINE
INCREASES WITH HIS INCOME

The data below from FirstMet shows how much a person's income affects their chances of being contacted online. For example, a man who lists his annual income over $150,000 has a 17.8% chance of being contacted by a woman.

17.8% CHANCE

11.6%
$20,000-
$40,000

13.1%
$40,000-
$60,000

13.7%
$60,000-
$80,000

15.5%
$80,000-
$150,000

$150,000
AND UP

INCOME FOR MEN

After the success of that story, we thought it would be fun to see which U.S. cities men are most likely to find gold diggers in.

WHERE THE FEMALE GOLD DIGGERS ARE?

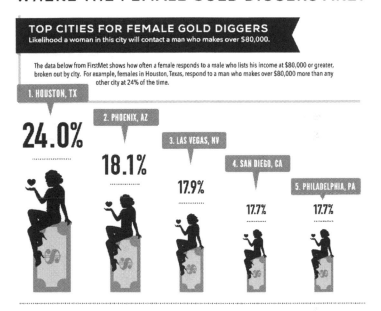

TOP CITIES FOR FEMALE GOLD DIGGERS
Likelihood a woman in this city will contact a man who makes over $80,000.

The data below from FirstMet shows how often a female responds to a male who lists his income at $80,000 or greater, broken out by city. For example, females in Houston, Texas, respond to a man who makes over $80,000 more than any other city at 24% of the time.

1. HOUSTON, TX
24.0%

2. PHOENIX, AZ
18.1%

3. LAS VEGAS, NV
17.9%

4. SAN DIEGO, CA
17.7%

5. PHILADELPHIA, PA
17.7%

SIZE MATTERS

Our data told us that everyone likes money and women prefer taller guys. Neither one of those statements were going to win us any accolades for a revolutionary discovery. However, both stories went viral because we were able to quantify the results and interpret them in an entertaining way. For example, every additional inch in height increased a guy's attractiveness, until 6'8". The key takeaway was that a man who is 6'2" is 57 percent more likely to be contacted than a man who is under 5'5".

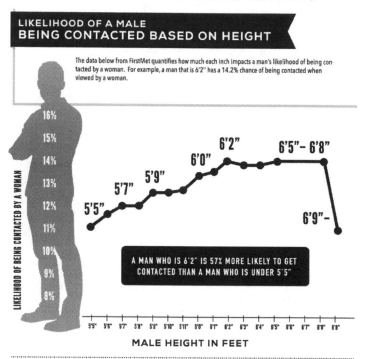

SIZE MATTERS IN ONLINE DATING

LIKELIHOOD OF A MALE BEING CONTACTED BASED ON HEIGHT

The data below from FirstMet quantifies how much each inch impacts a man's likelihood of being contacted by a woman. For example, a man that is 6'2" has a 14.2% chance of being contacted when viewed by a woman.

A MAN WHO IS 6'2" IS 57% MORE LIKELY TO GET CONTACTED THAN A MAN WHO IS UNDER 5'5"

LIKELIHOOD OF BEING CONTACTED BY A WOMAN

MALE HEIGHT IN FEET

The results were so interesting to us and our users that we decided to try running the same idea in the UK, our second largest market. Then we realized we could publish the story on many different geographic levels, so we localized the data down to the city. It turns out that guys who stood 5'9" or under living in Manhattan had only a 1.2 percent chance of being contacted by a female. This means that 99 out of 100 women would skip you at that height. However, in nearby Jersey City, short guys fared much better with a 7.6 percent *like* rate. Still not great, but I wondered if we could have caused a massive short-guy migration from Manhattan to Jersey City.

The bottom line is that we got massive coverage in *The Daily News* and *The New York Post* from that article, because we localized the story to the New York Metropolitan area.

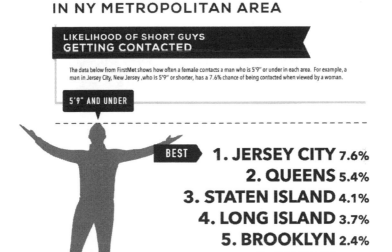

WHERE HEIGHT MATTERS MOST IN NY METROPOLITAN AREA

LIKELIHOOD OF SHORT GUYS GETTING CONTACTED

The data below from FirstMet shows how often a female contacts a man who is 5'9" or under in each area. For example, a man in Jersey City, New Jersey ,who is 5'9" or shorter, has a 7.6% chance of being contacted when viewed by a woman.

5'9" AND UNDER

BEST ▶ **1. JERSEY CITY** 7.6%
2. QUEENS 5.4%
3. STATEN ISLAND 4.1%
4. LONG ISLAND 3.7%
5. BROOKLYN 2.4%
6. BRONX 1.2%
WORST ▶ **7. MANHATTAN** 1.2%

WHERE DO CURVY WOMEN THRIVE?

Besides having a lot of fun with this data, we were genuinely trying to provide value to our users and readers. We know people tend to be very superficial online, so we thought it would be beneficial to see which cities prefer curvy women, while also identifying which cities were the most superficial.

THE BEST AND WORST CITIES
FOR CURVY WOMEN ONLINE

FirstMet examined **one hundred thousand** interactions to determine the best cities for curvy women based on the percentage of likes when a profile was viewed. For example, when a man in Las Vegas Nevada viewed a curvy woman's profile, she had a 12.1% chance of being liked.

BEST CITIES
Chances of getting liked if you are a curvy woman

1. LAS VEGAS, NV **12.1%**
2. PHILADELPHIA, PA **11.3%**
3. CLEVELAND, OH **11.2%**
4. LOS ANGELES, CA **9.1%**
5. HOUSTON, TX **8.9%**

WORST CITIES
Chances of getting liked if you are a curvy woman

1. SAN JOSE, CA **1.1%**
2. SEATTLE, WA **1.3%**
3. DALLAS, TX **2.8%**
4. NEW YORK, NY **2.9%**
5. PHOENIX, AZ **3.5%**

RACIAL PROFILING

OkCupid released a great story on racial factors in online dating. It was very controversial, but that's what we were going for as well. We wondered if we could take that concept (which had been executed a few years prior) and update it with much more robust data on a more granular level, specifically quantifying how much each ethnicity got liked and disliked by gender.

That story became front page news, mostly due to a fun and catchy data point. Asian women are the most preferred by all men except Asian men, who actually prefer Hispanic women.

By including both genders, the story became relevant for everybody, which helped the story spread. We even got press coverage from many different television networks from it. The experience taught us that most of these stories could be updated and reproduced every few years. They didn't need to be original, because the passage of time can make them compelling again. After three years have passed, it's likely that an entirely different online dating audience will be reading the stories for the first time. Here were some of the more interesting findings that fed the media frenzy (which we tagged with a catchy title), mostly due to their controversial nature in providing data to prove or disprove preconceptions:

- Asian women are the most preferred by all men except Asian men, who prefer Hispanic women.
- Asian, Hispanic, and Caucasian women prefer Caucasian men, while Caucasian men are more likely to respond to everyone except Caucasian women.
- Caucasian women are twice as likely to respond to Caucasian men than African-American men.
- African-American women are 34 percent more likely than any other race to respond to a man online, while Asian women are the least likely to respond.

Once that story was successful, we thought it would be interesting to combine stories that were separately successful, like ethnicity and body type. Specifically, we analyzed how different ethnicities responded to women who label themselves as "curvy." This helped both stories continue to gain momentum and kept them in the news for a while. Some interesting results were:

- Asian men are most likely to "like" curvy women with a 15 percent "like" rate.
- Caucasian men are the least likely to "like" curvy women.
- Asian men are 85 percent more likely than Caucasian men to "like" curvy women.
- African-American men are 52 percent more likely than Caucasian men to "like" curvy women.

- Hispanic men are 28 percent more likely than Caucasian men to "like" curvy women.
- Men of all ethnicities prefer slender or toned women.

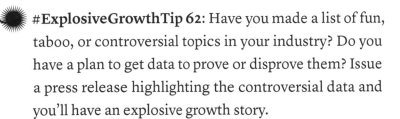 **#ExplosiveGrowthTip 62:** Have you made a list of fun, taboo, or controversial topics in your industry? Do you have a plan to get data to prove or disprove them? Issue a press release highlighting the controversial data and you'll have an explosive growth story.

THE BEAUTY OF THE TOP TEN LIST

Another secret ingredient we learned to get these data stories to go viral was to frame the title as a numbered list, such as a top five, ten, or more list. Consider some of the following lists we wrote about:

- Top Ten Best and Worst Cities for Singles Over Forty
- Top Five Cities Where Women Want Casual Relationships
- Top Five Cities Where Men Want Serious Relationships

RINGS AND FLINGS

WHERE WOMEN WANT TO HOOK UP AND MEN WANT TO GET HITCHED

FirstMet analyzed nearly 1.6 million responses to the question, "Are you looking for a serious relationship, or something casual?", and the results led us to some interesting conclusions about singles in the United States. Women want commitment and men want no strings attached, right? That may not be the case, according to the data.

THE FLINGS
Top 5 Cities Where Women Want Casual Relationships

1. LOUISVILLE, KY
2. MILWAUKEE, WI
3. LOS ANGELES, CA
4. SACRAMENTO, CA
5. DETROIT, MI

1. BOSTON, MA
2. FORT WORTH, TX
3. MEMPHIS, TN
4. MIAMI, FL
5. FORT LAUDERDALE, FL

THE RINGS
Top 5 Cities Where Men Want Serious Relationshps

By breaking down the information into these short, digestible chunks of numerical information, the reader is drawn to the story. So many companies try so hard to get one story to go viral, but I feel like we cracked the code. For us, it wasn't a matter of *if* a story was going to go viral, it was a matter of *when do we want* the next story to go viral.

#ExplosiveGrowthTip 63: Schedule a company brainstorming session to come up with ideas for a top ten list about your industry or product.

THE CONTINUED EFFECTIVENESS OF NEWSJACKING

Newsjacking is taking a trending news item and injecting the company into the conversation to generate media coverage and social media engagement. Previously, we had newsjacking success with the Duke basketball story and the Britney Spears situation. Those were trending stories where we added our own angle to it and got massive press as a result.

The beauty of newsjacking is that the story is already trending (which means it will likely have a lot of follow-up stories), and it's not time consuming to come up with an angle. Putting out an entire press release isn't necessary. All that's needed is to send the writers the particular angle and/or data points. An added benefit is that large companies can't really compete in real time, because newsjacking requires a speed they can't match. For all these reasons, a little time invested in newsjacking can provide the potential for a big ROI.

Another benefit of newsjacking is that the topics tend to repeat themselves. Think about presidential elections, severe weather, and other stories that inevitably resurface every so often. So, being prepared and anticipating the story can be very valuable. For example, extreme weather such as a snowstorm will always be a periodically trending story ripe for newsjacking. So, whenever a snowstorm was predicted, we would immediately provide data to reporters that showed how users flock to dating sites during a storm, likely looking for a "cuddle buddy." We used data to show that messaging activity increased 340 percent during the prior year's storm. Using this method, we were able to inject ourselves into a national news story about severe weather at least once per year.

#ExplosiveGrowthTip 64: Have you identified trending news stories that you can inject your company into? Are you actively providing the writers with a new angle or fresh data?

#ExplosiveGrowthTip 65: Anticipate newsjacking opportunities by identifying upcoming concerts, festivals, sporting events, conferences, annual events, and trade shows. Do you have a list of at least three upcoming opportunities for newsjacking?

#ExplosiveGrowthTip 66: Speed is key and the big boys can't keep up. Have you contacted key writers to tell them you will provide any data and survey information they need within a tight timeframe?

10

TINDER CRACKS THE CODE

"If you use your money to create exceptional products and services, you won't need to spend it on advertising."

—SETH GODIN, AMERICAN AUTHOR AND
HIGHLY SUCCESSFUL ENTREPRENEUR

As soon as I heard about Tinder, I knew it was going to succeed. How did I know that? They found the Holy Grail of any product (especially an online dating site) which is growth through massive word-of-mouth. That type of growth not only costs nothing, but when a user learns about a product via referral from a friend, they're much more likely to embrace it than if a costly advertising campaign for it hits them in the face. For instance, I've heard of some $50,000 campaigns held during spring break with helicopters and girls in bikinis handing out flyers that got absolutely nothing in return. What a gaffe that would be!

"PLAYING TINDER"

The undeniable genius of Tinder first dawned on me when I was sitting at a bar in Manhattan one night. I noticed five or six women in their mid-twenties on their phones, looking like they were having a lot of fun. Judging from some of the reactions and bits and pieces of conversation I heard, it looked like they might have been using a dating app. I approached them to see which one they were using if that was the case.

I said, "Hi, do you mind if I ask what you're doing that looks like so much fun?"

One of them said, "Oh, we're playing this new game called Tinder."

With much more at stake than just a passing interest in the app world, I engaged them in a lively conversation to find out more about this new "game."

They explained to me that the app shows the user pictures of different men, one at a time. If the user likes the man, she swipes right. If the user doesn't like the man, she swipes left. Based on that explanation, I didn't fully understand the objective. So, I asked them how to win at a game like that.

They further explained, "You don't really win, but if the person you like also likes you, then you're matched, and you can then message each other and meet up."

I replied, "So, it *is* a dating site."

They argued that it was definitely *not* a dating site. Obviously, they preferred the concept of "playing a game" as opposed to the term, "online dating."

We went on to have a strangely animated debate back and forth about whether Tinder was a dating site, a game, or an online retail store with an inventory of available men. Finally, one of the girls got really frustrated and defensive, and she shouted, "No! We're not online dating! It's like we're shopping, but for men, get it?" That's when it occurred to me—Tinder was going to change the entire landscape of online dating. They'd cracked the code.

HOW DID THEY DO IT?

At that point in its existence, Tinder was not a household name, but I saw the "Wow!" factor immediately. I knew I needed to perform some research into what they were all about. As I said before, a lot of other dating apps were coming out around that time, and everybody thought I needed to pay attention to them. As it turns out, none of them were worth much of anything, and they all disappeared within twelve months or so. Tinder, however, I was justifiably concerned about.

NO MORE SECRET TABOO

Tinder figured out how to remove the secretive, taboo nature of online dating, which was prevalent in those days. Singles still weren't eager to share with friends that they were using online dating sites. This charming group of young women didn't think of Tinder as a representative of the online dating world. They thought of it as a game or a shopping experience, instead of any of the negative connotations associated with online dating. It was fun and acceptable to talk about Tinder with your friends, or to "play Tinder" as a group. After that night, I started to look around a little more when I went out, and I saw more and more groups of women "playing Tinder." That's when I realized we had a big problem.

I quickly called for an all-hands-on-deck meeting at SNAP Interactive, telling everybody, "There's a new dating app out there called Tinder, and it's going to be the biggest dating app in the world. We have to figure out what's going on." That led me to another realization. We eventually needed to build an app that had similar functionality, just to understand the power of some of those features. I was eager to integrate them into AYI, but then I recalled the lessons from our social discovery pivot. It would be just about impossible to effectively rebrand an existing product in the eyes of the user—we had to build an entirely new product. But first, we needed to understand why Tinder was gaining so much growth through simple word-of-mouth.

Compounding Tinder's effectiveness was that their user interface was awesome too. We had a good one, where a couple clicks would get a Facebook profile loaded and a new user signed on. On Tinder, however, a user was one click away from instantly seeing nearby attractive people. Do you like this person, yes or no? Done. That doesn't quite align with the principle of being ten times better, but it might have been five times better—still an improvement. It's not enough of an improvement on its own to make a big difference, but another aspect of Tinder's game-changing application definitely was.

In the online dating world—scratch that—in the dating world, guys are completely irrelevant. They just show up wherever the girls are. However, women want a good experience. Unfortunately, online dating—scratch that—dating can be a brutal experience for women. It's especially harsh in the online world. Women are constantly bombarded with unwanted messages from men they want nothing to do with. An app that could screen out non-matches for women was a Purple Cow. Tinder completely nailed this unmet need for women in online dating, because its functionality made it impossible to message another user unless you were a match.

This was a disruptive concept to the online dating world, because previously, sites were focused on simply getting the user as many messages as possible. Recall how our ninety-day sprint to increase revenue focused on getting more replies, which unwittingly resulted in an annoying level of unwanted pop-up messages for women.

For attractive women, messages from undesirable men were exceptionally problematic. It didn't matter if these women put in their searches that they were only interested in guys named Troy or Lance who were over six feet tall with the body of a professional athlete and a seven-figure income to match. They would still get inundated with messages from unemployed accountants named Irv or Larry who were five-foot-two inches tall with a receding hairline and living in their grandmother's basement. By not allowing unwanted messages, Tinder's functionality was at least ten times better—they had really cracked the code. Anytime a woman received a message, she knew it would be from somebody she'd liked, which was a magical experience.

THE SOONER, THE BETTER

AYI did a great job of improving the user experience for people who were accustomed to online dating through the more popular traditional sites, where it would take days or weeks to get a date. We could do it much quicker than that. However, Tinder had functionality to do that better too. Remember how Facebook used supporting technology like digital cameras to add to their experience? Tinder used GPS functionality.

While users "play Tinder," the app leverages the GPS functionality on their phones to show them profiles of potential matches closest to them. If a user likes someone who likes them back, they could meet in mere minutes if they were close enough. This was another instance of Tinder doing something ten times better.

I ran an experiment with several of my friends—guys and

gals—to verify that Tinder was really ten times better than other online dating sites at meeting someone quickly. After all, the initial objective of users on a dating site is to get a date. I asked them to try a variety of online dating apps to see how quickly they could get a date on each one. With zero exceptions, all of them came back with the same result: Tinder allowed them to meet someone more quickly than any other site. Most of them met someone on Tinder within two hours, as opposed to two or more days on the other websites. In other words, Tinder's ability to deliver on the core user objective, a date, was literally ten times faster than other dating sites. Game, set, match to Tinder.

 #ExplosiveGrowthTip 67: Can you quantify how much superior your core product offering is than the competition? Is it 10X better?

AN IMPROVED CALL-TO-ACTION (CTA)

Evidently, the founders of Tinder understood all about the previous taboo nature of online dating. They knew they had to remove the stigma that sat like a glowing red scarlet letter on every online dating website's CTA button, which usually read something like, "Browse More Singles!" The reason the first group of women I ran into at the bar said they were "playing Tinder" was most likely because Tinder's CTA button asked, "Keep Playing?" It was a brilliantly shrewd use of language that made users think they were playing a game, rather than online dating.

I could see that all these brilliant features combined with their growth rocket was going to take Tinder to a level of success that AYI was never going to achieve. It was very frustrating for me, but there wasn't much I could do about it. As I've said before, you only get one chance to make a first impression.

AYI was already everything it was going to be in the minds of most users. In fact, by that time, its interface wasn't all that different from Tinder. They get credit (along with Hinge) for being the first apps to feature that swipe left or right technology and introducing mutual friends and interests, but we actually implemented those features several years earlier. Another problem was that we were a paid app, which eliminated our ability to engage that same college-level and younger target audience that Tinder was having huge success with—the audience crucial to getting the elusive and extremely valuable word-of-mouth growth.

11

MY INNOVATOR'S DILEMMA

"If a product's future is unlikely to be remarkable—if you can't imagine a future in which people are once again fascinated by your product—it's time to realize that the game has changed. Instead of investing in a dying product, take profits and reinvest them in building something new."

—SETH GODIN, AMERICAN AUTHOR AND
HIGHLY SUCCESSFUL ENTREPRENEUR

Once I had the chance to fully absorb the implications of Tinder, it became very clear to me I needed to figure out how SNAP Interactive could go back to being innovators instead of followers. As my friend Andrew once told me, when a fast-growing new product is based upon a disruptive technology (Tinder leveraging GPS to show potential matches nearby), people tend to underestimate how quickly the established leaders will decline (think Friendster and Myspace after Facebook arrived). I experienced this when AYI was launched on Facebook and introduced several disruptive online dating features, which decimated the traffic for Hot or Not and several other established dating leaders. That memory made me justifiably concerned that Tinder's emergence might have put us on the wrong side of that equation. But even if we could have foreseen Tinder's rapid rise, what could we have done about it?

I sought inspiration for this problem the same way I did with most other business crises I've faced—I read a book. Over the course of one particularly uneventful weekend, I read *The Innovator's Dilemma: When New Technologies Cause Great Firms to Fail,* by Clayton M. Christensen. That book is the foremost authority on how large, established companies can remain relevant and continue to innovate.

Immediately after I finished reading it, I was wishing I'd read that book a few years earlier, because so many problems we'd experienced had become painfully obvious to me. Sharing resources such as funds, people, and even an office, along with your core products and new opportunities usually leads to a sub-optimal result for the new opportunity. Here are a few reasons why our initial attempts at innovating with a new product failed:

- **The core product needs constant attention.** If the core product is declining, as was the case for AYI, there's always a new fire that needs to be put out. So, if resources are shared between the moneymaker and the new initiative, all the time and attention will go back to the core product to put out the 'fire.' It's impossible to justify keeping people on a new initiative that won't pay the bills for a while, as long as the moneymaker is suffering.

- **KPIs are comparatively demoralizing.** What looks like a huge win for the innovative product team, will look comparatively feeble to the rest of the organization.

- **The best people need to be working on the biggest opportunities, not the biggest problems.** With our core product driving 100 percent of the revenues, yet in serious decline, it was counter-intuitive to take our best people away from it. However, if we hadn't done that, the innovation required to succeed on a new initiative would never have materialized.

- **Talented people are always looking for new challenges, and it's the CEOs job to keep them hungry.**

Reversing the bleeding for AYI and scratching out 3 to 5 percent gains, although interesting enough to me, because it meant around $1 million in incremental profits, it wasn't interesting to talented engineers who sought a career challenge more than financial prosperity. Remember, money doesn't drive most talented people, especially engineers and product managers. By continuing to have them focus on small ideas, it was uninteresting and demotivating for them. After all, there are only so many colors to test for a button.

 #ExplosiveGrowthTip 68: Are your most talented people working on the biggest opportunities instead of the biggest problems?

- **Financial resources for the new initiatives must be separated.** As our core business continued to decline, it became very difficult to justify spending money on the new initiative. The biggest reason was that the core product had clear and immediate ROIs on any incremental investment, but the new product was an unknown, and thus had no measurable ROIs. However, one thing was well-known with the new product. Any incremental investment would increase the company's burn rate and create more financial stress. It was nearly impossible for a lot of people to understand (and who could blame them?) why we had layoffs, yet we continued to spend money on experimental initiatives that had no tangible returns coming anytime soon. The best way to plan for such a problem is to have a separate bank account with money exclusively earmarked for the new initiative. That way, if an uncontrollable urge strikes to reduce investment in the new product, at least it's a lot more difficult to do, since the capital is tucked away in a separate account.

#ExplosiveGrowthTip 69: When creating a new product, create a separate account with funds earmarked exclusively for the new initiative. Do you have different accounts for different products?

A bunch of case studies throughout Christensen's book describe how some companies overcame those critical issues and more. The gist of the book told me that I basically needed to recreate a start-up within my own company to solve our issues and create new and innovative products. I needed a dedicated staff, complete with their own clearly defined budget and unique KPIs to work on the innovation of new products and nothing else. I would also need to shift top performers to work on the largest opportunities, instead of the largest problems. That was going to be a challenge, since the largest opportunity equated to zero short-term revenue.

START-UP 2.0

I showed up for work that Monday morning and immediately called a meeting. Most of my staff realized when I did that, it meant I had done some reading over the weekend. At the meeting, I explained how we needed to start something fresh, and we had to do it with a dedicated team. Initially, they didn't like that idea very much, but they understood why it needed to happen. Eventually, their acceptance of the need to start something new meant I could get excited about innovation again. That justified me getting out of the humdrum, day-to-day CEO responsibilities of trying to squeeze every last drop of revenue I could out of AYI and put it back into my entrepreneurial spirit.

With the passion for innovation burning anew in my creative heart once again, I approached Alex Harrington (my COO at the time) with an offer. I wanted him to take over as CEO. I wanted to focus 100 percent of my efforts on building the new product. I knew it needed my undivided attention to have a good shot at success. I also decided to take a 50 percent pay cut, and use those extra funds for the new initiative to further align the project like a start-up. I was very fortunate he said, "Yes." Besides being a very talented executive, he already had in-depth experience running an online dating site called MeetMoi (which had been bought by Match.com).

Once again, great talent provided a big advantage for the company. Outwardly, this looked like a major change. But internally, it was a seamless transition, because we tapped into a ripe resource of an existing talent who was already familiar with all the responsibilities of being a CEO and especially, the inner workings of SNAP. That action also greatly helped to get the message across to the rest of the company that the new product was a serious effort of utmost importance.

WOMEN DON'T LIKE TO BE HARASSED ONLINE (DUH!)

We had to understand what was so compelling about these new swiping apps, so we created something that built upon Tinder's simplicity and approach to the female user experience, which we called, Mutually. Ironically enough, Mutually was essentially a replica of the AYI of old—the free AYI—with a couple of tweaks.

Right away, the data showed us what we had suspected all along. The experience for women was infinitely better, because they weren't getting unwanted messages from guys who looked like their best friend's weird cousin, Derek, when they were looking for guys who looked more like Derek Jeter. The retention was great, but with Tinder exploding at this point, we knew we needed to have a major differentiator—a Purple Cow.

~~DICK PICS~~

Around the same time when we were trying to reinvent ourselves with a new product, some female friends of mine were telling me about inappropriate pictures and messages that they had received while using the newly popular mobile dating apps. Three of these friends had received something not-so-affectionately known in the online dating world as the "dick pic." Of course, accompanying the dick pick was usually some written content crude enough to make Madonna blush. For the most part, guys have no shame, no idea what's acceptable for communication, and delusions of grandeur when it comes to the opposite sex.

Adding fuel to this lecherous fire, we learned it had become a game with users who wanted to see how many matches they could get, which basically meant that men would like (swipe right) on every girl (as a matter of fact, nearly 50 percent of men do swipe-right on every girl). In order to compete in this game, men would send very provocative messages in order to 'stand out from the crowd' and get a response, Unfortunately, this strategy did achieve the initial goal in getting responses from women, albeit not a flattering one for the most part. Thus, the degrading experience for women on the new crop of swiping apps was still happening, despite the online dating world's best efforts to keep it away.

We conducted a survey that attempted to quantify this need to provide a better, safer, and significantly less disgusting online dating experience for women. The result was that 90 percent of females on mobile dating apps responded that they had received the questionably comical, but definitely lewd and distasteful "dick pic" or similar type of reference at some point. The overwhelming prevalence of such behavior simply blew us away.

From this survey, we began the company's brainstorming process once again. We had this new swiping app that had some promising numbers to start with. Also, we had a response rate of 90 percent of female users pleading for a solution to their online dating horrors.

The question was, "How do we take advantage of this information?" It didn't take long for the answer to surface. We needed to figure out a way to hold users accountable (especially guys) for their online dating behavior. We needed to remove the creeps from online dating, and we needed to offer a solution that would create a safe, respectful online dating experience, where there would be ramifications for behavior that didn't make "The Grade." We believed our elusive Purple Cow would provide a remarkable experience for women, and as we had already learned, they were all that really mattered.

MONEY TROUBLES

Unfortunately, while this revelation struck, the company was mired in a stock slump. Tinder was absolutely on fire, and our numbers were still declining. It became clear at this point that we needed to raise more money if the new product was ever going to get off the ground and the existing product was going to survive.

We had made great progress on the new initiatives, and our analytics were still considered the gold standard in the industry. However, the revenues were declining—leading to a poorly performing stock. That made it very difficult to find new capital on acceptable terms. Ultimately, we were able to raise another $3 million in convertible debt, but the terms included a lot of harsh restrictions and covenants.

One of those terms stated if the cash in our bank accounts dropped below a certain level, we would have to pay the debt back sooner. So, even though we had more money, we really couldn't touch most of it without major penalties. That type of structure and pressure severely conflicted with investing in a new product and prioritizing its long-term growth ahead of short-term revenue considerations.

The firm that invested in us assured us they would support our growth ambitions and they would reconsider those restrictions if the numbers supported it. Despite their encouraging words of support, we still negotiated heavily to relax the restrictions even further. Unfortunately, our negotiations were mostly fruitless, and we were ultimately stuck with them and had no other financing options.

#ExplosiveGrowthTip 70: Make sure any potential investors are fully aligned with your strategy and vision. Talk to the companies behind their failing prior investments to see how the investors behaved when the going got tough.

#ExplosiveGrowthTip 71: Raising debt can be very dangerous. Try to avoid it entirely, if possible.

Nonetheless, with restrictions and covenants tugging on our collective coattails, we proceeded with the new business venture. A brilliant idea was brewing, and we were ready to release a new product that addressed the major pain point for women in online dating. It's not often that more than one Purple Cow surfaces in a company.

12

MAKING "THE GRADE"

"To launch a business means successfully solving problems.
Solving problems means listening."

—RICHARD BRANSON, WILDLY SUCCESSFUL
ENTREPRENEUR, INVESTOR, AND PHILANTHROPIST

The concept for The Grade came from an attempt to satisfy a woman's need to have a superior online dating experience, free of creeps. We described The Grade as a community of high-quality singles who were not only desirable, but also articulate and respectful.

We created an algorithm that graded users based on several factors, including the quality and content of their

EXPLOSIVE GROWTH · 265

messages. Something as out-of-bounds as a dick pic, or any type of inappropriate sexual suggestion or reference would seriously affect your score. It turned out that poor grammar and spelling were also huge turnoffs for women, so we took points off for those items as well.

If your grade fell into the bottom 10 percent of the user base, you would receive an "F," and you would be put on a short probation. If your behavior didn't improve, you would be permanently banned from the site. With this system in place, The Grade became the first online dating site to truly hold users accountable for their behavior.

#ExplosiveGrowthTip 72: Focus on building solutions to problems, rather than building new products or features.

At launch, The Grade took off like a rocket. There were dozens of articles written about it in major publications, such as the *Wall Street Journal, Buzzfeed, ABC News, USA Today, Time Magazine, The New York Post, Refinery29, Cosmopolitan,* and *Vogue,* which added to its quick rise in popularity.

All the lessons we learned from the need for a USP, making great use of data and leveraging controversial or taboo items proved extremely valuable in reaching our female target audience. We continued to use data stories to boost The Grade's popularity and nearly every story went viral.

YOUR MEDIA PAGE MATTERS

Understanding that press was going to be very important from the outset of The Grade's launch, we were sure to incorporate a robust media page on our website that included some key items:

- An easy link to download the app
- Compelling product messaging about why the app is unique
- Data around the site's impressive usage
- A story about the founders
- A fun story about the product's origin
- High-resolution screenshots
- Video footage of how to use the product
- An entertaining FAQ
- Social proof (quotes from major media outlets)
- An easy to way to contact us

Not letting the media page get static or bland was very important, so we kept updating it. Every time we got a social media hit, we added a reference to it at the bottom of the page, which provided verifiable social proof of our influence.

 #ExplosiveGrowthTip 73: Do you have all your media and product information (listed above) easily accessible on one page online for the media to access anytime?

GET LUCKY BY BEING PREPARED

"Luck Is Created by The Prepared."

—JAMES ALTUCHER, AMERICAN ENTREPRENEUR
AND BEST-SELLING AUTHOR

There was one instance when we got a call from a top television news station who wanted to mention The Grade on the prime-time nightly news—they needed some information and data about the product within the hour. I pointed them to our media page on the website with the screenshots, product background, and video clips. With everything they could possibly want already available, they ended up creating a much larger segment on the nightly news, which garnered us thousands of users in NYC.

We got a lot more opportunities for publicity solely by making it easier for the press to find what they needed from us, including high-resolution images and video clips about the product. The press was always operating within a tight deadline, so by giving them quick access to key pieces of information and media content, they could run stories on the company easily and efficiently.

On a few occasions, the press was looking to talk to users of the app. We learned the hard way that trying to find users who we were comfortable with representing our brand within a tight deadline was nearly impossible. To prevent this from being an ongoing problem, we planned ahead and lined up a few "users" (who may or may not have been friends of mine) who would be willing to talk to the media anytime. As a result, we would get "lucky" many times over because of being prepared and making it super easy for the media.

 #ExplosiveGrowthTip 74: Do you have a few "friendly users" on standby, ready to speak positively about your product to the media?

SOCIALIZE

Another thing we understood before launching The Grade was the value of socializing with writers. Members of the press are like anybody else—they play favorites. We lost some opportunities for publicity with AYI, because we didn't have a network of writers on standby, ready to boast about our product, a new feature, or an exciting business development. With that knowledge in hand, we lined up an exclusive budget for The Grade, to be used to regularly meet with key writers who could build relationships and continue sharing our product's vision. That strategy paid off handsomely when we came out with product updates, and it got us substantial coverage, because the writers were familiar with the team and our product.

#ExplosiveGrowthTip 75: Have a meet-and-greet at your office with key reporters and bloggers. The most social employees should be there to mingle and show off what they're working on. Have you met personally with key reporters yet?

THE VALUE OF GOOD PR

Data stories, socializing with key writers, and having a robust media page were all part of one very crucial aspect of launching and growing our new product, which was PR. On a more granular level, we also had a great PR team working for us, led by Adam Handelsman of SpecOps Communications, who knew the industry well, and he knew how the news cycle worked.

While basking in the sun and fun of South Beach, Florida on vacation one weekend, I received a call from my PR guy, who told me that Fox News wanted to schedule me for a live television appearance in a couple of hours. It was a fantastic opportunity, but I was in South Beach and there was no way I was going to be able to make it to the interview, which was thousands of miles away, in time. They suggested we do a Skype interview, but for various reasons that wasn't going to be a viable option either. The power of my having hired great talent once again worked in my favor, because my PR guy convinced them to reschedule the interview by saying, "If we reschedule this for the Sunday Night edition instead, we'll be able to prepare better, and we'll be able to present you with more updated and compelling information." They said, "Oh, we like that idea. Let's do it!"

Our PR machine was firing on all cylinders, and we had a massively successful launch of The Grade. We just needed to continue that positive momentum and grow the product.

#NOMORECREEPS

One of our goals before launch was to be mentioned in the same breath as Tinder, and we accomplished that. I kept track of how many articles mentioned us when talking about Tinder to track our progress. A lot of press was touting our model of "no more creeps" as the alternative to Tinder, and magazines like *Cosmo* and *Vogue* wrote about us because they loved that concept. It was our USP or Purple Cow that attracted the most crucial target audience for a dating site (women), because as I explained earlier, they are all who mattered.

Understanding that women were the key, and when we

provided them with a safe environment, it was the perfect way to attract them to our site. We expanded on that ideal by grading users with a feature called "Peer Review." That feature allowed users to give a thumbs-up or thumbs-down to other users based on their interactions with them.

To ensure the ratings weren't affected by spite after a bad date or by an ex looking to trash someone's reputation, we used a weighting system based on the extent of the relationship (whether they were Facebook friends, quantity of messages sent, etc.). In case a user had been the target of some bad faith, just a few thumbs-down wouldn't necessarily hurt them. On the other hand, if a user had a lot of thumbs-down indicators, then that would weigh quite heavily.

That functionality became one part of a unique three-part grading system that assigned a traditional letter grade (A-F) based on three aspects of a user's membership—profile, messaging, and peer review.

All the magical metrics were positive for The Grade—a true USP, a great NPS, and a wonderful retention rate that I had never seen in any dating site before, including AYI in its heyday. But the team was so tiny, and we were competing against brands like Tinder and another rapidly growing competitor (Bumble), both of which had massive resources behind them. Those resource-rich competitors also had the advantage of being able to focus entirely on one product. We needed to grow our team and invest in the product, but we still had to support AYI, which presented a big problem.

SEPARATE BUT UNFORTUNATELY EQUAL

Because The Grade was dragging AYI along like a wounded soldier on the battlefield, we struggled just to keep the current budget justified. Whereas marketing dollars spent on AYI generated immediate revenue, marketing dollars spent on The Grade were still only generating Instagram followers and installs. I also didn't want to repeat the mistakes I had made with AYI—like charging for a product too soon, especially while our competitors were offering their products for free.

Increasing the budget for The Grade was impossible as we didn't want to fall below the cash covenants in our debt agreement. If we crossed that threshold, we would have to start paying the money back sooner, and our cash would have been depleted even faster—a death spiral.

Unfortunately, when we went to private investors for more money, they kept giving us the same response: "If The Grade was its own separate company, we'd be all over it, because the user growth and retention numbers were quite impressive. But, because it's tied into the performance of AYI, and you're already publicly traded, we can't justify investing in it." On the other hand, public company investors were only interested in revenue growth, and it was way too soon to start charging, so they had no interest either, because all they saw was the overall revenue in decline due to the beaten horse that was AYI.

This was one of the most frustrating things I ever experienced—we were sitting on what I believed was a goldmine in our new and exciting product with all the right metrics to support it (and savvy venture capitalists agreed), but we were completely beholden to AYI, which was old and uninteresting to investors.

#ExplosiveGrowthTip 76: The corporate setup is crucial. For us, being publicly traded had some advantages, but in the end, it hurt us far more often than it helped. Are there any structural issues with your company setup that are holding you back, and are you addressing them now?

The metrics for The Grade were far superior to those from start-ups that were all raising $10 million or even $20 million, but it didn't matter, because The Grade was buried within this larger organization. Because we were a public company, any path we took would have required serious legal work, shareholder goading, and a whole host of complex and costly acts totaling more than $1 million. It also would have involved a substantial investment of precious executive time that was already stretched too thin. That was just to start the process, and then we would have needed to go through the additional process of raising money. It just didn't make a lot of sense, no matter how we looked at it.

Our company's total marketing budget at that time was around $5 million, with only about 5 percent of that dedicated to The Grade. Unfortunately, we had to cut it even more because of the restrictions imposed by our recent capital raise.

With a shrinking budget, our marketing efforts had to be smarter than ever to promote growth. One of the ways we did that was by creating even more compelling data stories to attract people to the website. We also made effective use of specifically targeted blogs and influencer marketing.

DATA STORIES 2.0

It only made sense to leverage our expertise in manufacturing fun, readable, and effective data to promote growth for The Grade, the same way we did with AYI. In fact, by the time The Grade hit its stride in popularity, the data stories for it were much better than anything we had ever done with AYI.

A Picture is Worth a Thousand Dates

We thought it was important to continue to distinguish ourselves from the shallowness of most dating sites. My next idea concerned user photos.

I firmly believed that if people had photos that showed their personality, a user didn't need to be a supermodel or a professional athlete to get attention. We did two things to prove this.

First, we made it easy for users to see which photos performed best, by giving them data for each picture they uploaded in a feature called 'Photo Stats.' Although it was brutally honest, users loved it, because we discovered that most users were shockingly oblivious about what constituted a good or bad photo. Although, in hindsight, perhaps this shouldn't have been so shocking, considering so many men previously thought that snapping a picture of their gigglestick was a good idea.

I knew Photo Stats was going to be a huge success, because it satisfied something that always makes for a great product or feature, which is to take an action that people are already doing in an inefficient manner, and make it ten times easier for them to get the results they want. In this case, users on dating sites were always trying new photos in an attempt to see which photos got the most messages. But that was very difficult to accomplish without actual data that proves the superior performance on one photo over another. By displaying to the user how often each photo got liked or skipped, we had a 10X feature that provided massive value to the user. Since launching Photo Stats, we've seen several other dating sites incorporate something similar.

Next, we wrote a data story that quantified the importance of posting photos that brought out a person's unique personality. We went through tens of thousands of photos and categorized them (travel, playing sports, playing an instrument, with a pet, etc.), and compared each photo's performance to the user's average photo "like" rate. We poignantly titled it, "What Does Your Photo Say About You?"

The data showed us some interesting facts that users loved, and the story went viral immediately. We were proving that if users took time to take interesting photos that showed off their personalities, they would get much better matches in return, and they didn't need to be Brad Pitt or Scarlett Johansson.

One of the more polarizing photo categories was pictures that included dogs. Men who posed with a dog in their profile picture were seen as nurturing, (which women evidently found endearing) and received a 29 percent increase in likes. Conversely, if a woman posed with a dog in her profile picture, men viewed it as a distraction. They extrapolated that women would see them as second fiddle to their fur baby, wouldn't give them the attention they desired, and would end the date at a "reasonable" time with little chance for extracurricular activities. Way to go guys. Not only are a lot of us creeps, but we're also hopelessly needy—a dog in a female user's profile pic resulted in a 19 percent decrease in likes.

Take a look at the full results here:

A PICTURE IS WORTH 1,000 WORDS: WHAT DOES YOUR PROFILE PHOTO SAY ABOUT YOU?

WOMEN		MEN	
Instrument	+29%	Pro Head Shot	+92%
Sports Activity	+21%	Facial Hair	+57%
Bikini	+8%	Dog	+29%
Formal Wear	+8%	Travel	+23%
Hat	+5%	Instrument	+17%
Selfie	+2%	Not Smiling	+16%
Cleavage	+1%	Sports Activity	+13%
Pro Head Shot	+1%	Sunglasses	+12%
Travel	+1%	Eye Glasses	+1%
Not Looking	0%	Selfie	0%
Not Smiling	0%	Alcohol	-6%
Sunglasses	0%	Tattoos	-8%
Alcohol	-6%	Shirtless	-15%
Group Photo	-13%	Stadium/Arena	-16%
Eye Glasses	-14%	Formal Wear	-21%
Dog	-19%	Not Looking	-21%
Stadium/Arena	-21%	Hat	-25%
Tattoos	-35%	Group	-33%

This story seemed to really strike a chord with a lot of users, because people were always uploading new photos. So, it was interesting for them to discover what constituted a good photo for an online dating profile. Many people— correctly or not—view a swiping dating app as a contest of who the hottest user is. I think this data story, however, proves that interesting can still do very well.

Guys get a bad rap quite often for being superficial, but the top two categories of interest for profile pictures of women were playing an instrument/singing (which led to a 29 percent increase in likes from men) and sports (which leads to a 21 percent increase in likes).

Contrary to popular belief, I guess we do think about more than just sex when we're looking at women. Of course, the third one is a bikini shot (sigh), so we won't take too much credit for this revelation, but still, two out of three isn't bad, right?

What's In A Name? About 500 Million Page Views

I became obsessed with knowing what factors made a data story go viral. It became very clear it had nothing to do with random occurrences or luck. More research was needed, and that's when I found a book called, *Contagious: Why Things Catch On* by Jonah Berger.

The book provides a thorough explanation of why stories go viral by analyzing numerous stories and attributing their success to a breakdown of six principles. That book really influenced me—I figured out how I could apply those six principles to almost anything and get a story to go viral—which is exactly how I approached the next data story about names.

A friend of mine tried to set me up on a date with a girl

named Alexis. I politely asked, "Cool, does she go by Lexi or Alexis?" She replied, "Oh, she actually prefers Lexi." I said, "Great!" A little surprised by my exuberance, she asked, "Why do you ask?" I said, "Well, anytime you meet a girl named Lexi, she's attractive. If she goes by Alexis though, it could go either way." That moment of ridiculous and totally unfounded speculation gave me an idea for the next data story: what was the "like" rate on The Grade for certain names?

HOTTEST FEMALE NAMES				HOTTEST MALE NAMES		
	Name	% of Guys Who Swiped Right	Most Matched Name		Name	% of Girls Who Swiped Right	Most Matched Name
1	Brianna	70%	Sean	1	Brett	24%	Jessica
2	Erika	69%	Joe	2	Tyler	23%	Jennifer
3	Lexi	67%	Chris	3	Corey	23%	Amy
4	Brooke	65%	Mike	4	Andy	23%	Maria
5	Vanessa	65%	Tyler	5	Noah	23%	Elizabeth
6	April	63%	Tom	6	Shane	22%	Taylor
7	Natalie	63%	Jonathan	7	Jeffrey	21%	Michelle
8	Jenna	62%	Christopher Joseph	8	Rob	20%	Sarah
9	Molly	62%		9	Frank	20%	Stephanie
10	Katie	61%	Eddie	10	Jeff	20%	Emily
11	Laura	60%	Bobby	11	Zack	20%	Amanda
12	Rebecca	60%	Jeremy	12	Brandon	19%	Liz
13	Lindsey	60%	Daniel	13	Nicholas	19%	Amy
14	Taylor	59%	Sean	14	Greg	19%	Danielle
15	Aly	59%	Andrew	15	Zachary	19%	Shannon

To see the entire list and where your name ranks, go to: http://www.explosive-growth. com/case-study.

This story started by trying to see if certain nicknames like Lexi (vs. Alexis), Ali (vs. Aly or Alison), Jenny (vs. Jen or Jennifer), Matt (vs. Matthew), or Dave (vs. David) rendered themselves to being more attractive than other names like Helga, Edna, Ralph, or Prometheus. However, the story evolved. I would never be so bold as to call this story statistically significant in any way, but it did end up striking an emotional chord with a lot of users. And my original speculation (that a girl named Lexi sounded more attractive than a girl named Alexis) was proven right!

Here are the results for which nicknames are hottest:

	HOTTEST FEMALE NICKNAMES			HOTTEST MALE NICKNAMES	
	Name	% of Guys Who Swiped Right		Name	% of Girls Who Swiped Right
Winner	Erika	69.10%	Winner	Michael	12.70%
	Erica	50.20%		Mike	12.60%
Winner	Rebecca	59.70%	Winner	Dave	18.60%
	Becky	22.50%		David	13.40%
Winner	Nikki	50.10%	Winner	Matthew	16.90%
	Nicole	45.90%		Matt	15.40%
Winner	Jen	54.30%	Winner	Jonathan	13.80%
	Jennifer	44.90%		Jon	8.30%
Winner	Sarah	53.70%		Johnny	13.50%
	Sara	45.20%		Jon	10.10%
Winner	Aly	59.00%	Winner	Rick	17.10%
	Allison	57.50%		Richard	7.00%
	Ali	51.50%		Ricky	15.50%
	Allie	50.40%	Winner	Jeffrey	20.90%
Winner	Elizabeth	58.90%		Jeff	20.00%
	Liz	47.60%	Winner	Josh	12.10%
Winner	Katie	60.80%		Joshua	7.40%
	Kathleen	59.00%	Winner	Steve	13.20%
	Kat	47.10%		Steven	12.60%
	Cat	54.00%		Stephen	11.70%
Winner	Lexi	67.00%	Winner	Christopher	16.70%
	Alexis	41.30%		Chris	14.80%
			Winner	Rob	20.40%
				Robert	10.30%

ONE SMOKIN' HOT BRIANNA MAY HAVE SKEWED THESE NUMBERS

Full disclosure about data stories related to The Grade: Because The Grade was a relatively new product, we didn't have the same sample size to work with that we did for AYI. I remember with this story, there was one particularly attractive female user named Brianna who drew a "like" from just about any red-blooded, living and breathing male with eyes, so she single-handedly skewed the data. However, I would encourage some of the larger swiping sites (*ahem* Tinder) with a bigger user base to re-crunch the data and find out if Brianna and Brett are still the hottest names in online dating.

Specifically, the story went viral because it incorporated several of the six core principles Berger describes in his book: triggers (a person's name), emotion (according to Dale Carnegie's classic book, *How to Win Friends and Influence People*, your name is the most important sound to you), social currency, and practical value.

Book Recommendation: *Contagious: Why Things Catch On,* by Jonah Berger.

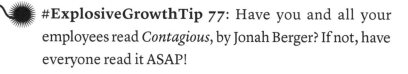 **#ExplosiveGrowthTip 77**: Have you and all your employees read *Contagious*, by Jonah Berger? If not, have everyone read it ASAP!

We ended up running the "like" rate for as many names

as we could find enough data for. Everyone wanted to see how hot their name was. Maybe it gave them an excuse to say something like, "Look, my name is Millhouse—there's only so much action out there for a guy named Millhouse." Or, maybe if their name was Millhouse, they could always change it to something like Stone, Brad, Fabio, or Beefcake. Regardless, our PR firm said that story got over a half-billion page views. That kind of reaction was more than just viral—more than contagious—it was positively pandemic!

HACKING YOUR WAY INTO LARGE BLOGS

There were two publications, *Refinery 29* and *Elite Daily*, with a predominantly female readership that shared a part of our core demographic: singles in their twenties and thirties. Those publications were very engaged with the dating world, but weren't giving us much coverage, despite the fact that we targeted them heavily.

Finally, one of our brainstorming sessions suggested that we try integrating those publications into a data story. Immediately, we thought to run some data that tried to quantify which blogs had the most attractive readers.

Fortunately, our suspicions were correct; *Refinery 29* and *Elite Daily* had the highest like rates among blog readers on our website, confirming that they had the most attractive readers. We ran with it, and Refinery29, Elite Daily, and every other blog that was mentioned featured the story.

WHICH BLOGS ARE THE HOTTEST SINGLES READING?

	LIKE RATE	USERS	PROFILE GRADE
Refinery29	64%	363	A+
Elite Daily	60%	586	A+
Jezebel	60%	92	A
Huffington Post	58%	419	A
Daily Mail	57%	64	A
Gawker	52%	141	A-
Mashable	51%	360	A-
Business Insider	50%	386	A-

 **#ExplosiveGrowthTip 78**: Find a fun and positive way to include your targeted blogs or influencers into a data story. They just may connect with you on it!

INFLUENCER MARKETING

Influencer marketing is all the rage these days, and for good reason. We caught on to that concept with The Grade when we aligned with some unique influencers on YouTube and Instagram to promote our product.

Most of these influencers were people who posted screenshots of guys being creeps on online dating sites. One woman, Lauren Urasek, was one of the most influential people in online dating, as she was rated the most popular person on OKCupid (she leveraged that into a book). Her vision aligned perfectly with ours, because she was all about a better online dating experience for women.

When Lauren appeared on *Good Morning America,* she spoke positively about us as an alternative to Tinder. This led to The Grade becoming the number one trending story on Facebook, the number one most-searched for term in the Apple app store, and got us thousands of new signups.

Through the heavy-duty marketing of controversial data stories, targeting the right blogs, and aligning ourselves with passionate influencers in our industry, The Grade sustained impressive word-of-mouth growth, despite a miniscule marketing budget. However, it was a struggle all the way.

Stress was bearing down from the recent capital raise, and there was a constant balancing act between the old product and the new (i.e., revenue vs. growth). It was a case of survival for AYI, while trying to make The Grade everything it could be. To sum it up, my corporate life at SNAP Interactive was as challenging as it had ever been.

Book Recommendation: *The Hard Thing About Hard Things: Building a Business When There Are No Easy Answers* by Ben Horowitz.

MY REBOOT

"The path to success is to take massive determined action."
—TONY ROBBINS, AMERICAN AUTHOR, ENTREPRENEUR,
PHILANTHROPIST, AND LIFE COACH

Not too long after stepping down as CEO and focusing solely on The Grade, a couple of life-changing events occurred that triggered a professional reboot for me.

The first event was on June 29, 2015, when my father—instrumental in the launch of the company—suddenly passed away. It was one of those major, transformative events that put everything into focus. It caused me to step back for a moment and reflect on what was truly important in my life. Not too long after that happened, I realized having fun and loving my work life was essential to not only my professional success, but also my personal satisfaction.

UNLEASHING MY POWER WITHIN

Once I came back to the office from a brief leave to grieve the loss of my father, I was understandably still in a funk from his passing. That's not the kind of event people get over simply by shifting into career mode. Sure, work took up a good portion of my time and kept my mind occupied, but it was still difficult for me to just take care of business and go forward without the man who'd had the greatest influence on who I had become.

My good friend Andrew Weinreich suggested going to a Tony Robbins seminar. He said it had changed his life dramatically many years earlier, and I remembered speaking with a few other very successful people who had similar experiences—so I decided to give it a try.

The seminar was called "Unleash the Power Within," and it proved to be the second life-changing event that greatly influenced my reboot. It was a three-day seminar that integrated some key exercises to gain mental clarity, sharper focus, and discover what made me passionate and feeling truly alive in order to achieve my life goals.

First on the agenda at this seminar was to achieve a peak state, which is a powerful and positive frame of mind that helps you live a more satisfying and fulfilling life. This exercise alone changed my life, because it took me back to moments where I was in a negative mindset, and it helped me see how my decisions were impacted accordingly. Once I realized how a negative mindset affected my decision making, the importance of being in a peak state when making crucial decisions dawned on me. Suddenly, I felt like I could conquer anything, and the quality of my decisions became much better.

While I was in that peak state, I became familiar with what Tony calls the ultimate success formula. This is where I explored in greater detail what exactly I wanted my outcome to be, what I was passionate about, and why. After this discovery process, I projected into the future and foreshadowed what my life would like look over the next few weeks, months, and years.

That glimpse of the future was a huge personal breakthrough—I saw how increasingly unhappy I was becoming, and it was only going to get worse as time went on. A big reason for this was that I wasn't sure how our company would regain our competitive advantage—its "economic moat" as Warren Buffet would call it. Our unique advantages from being very early on Facebook had eroded over the years, and now the network effect was working against us. Without those competitive advantages, our numbers would keep declining.

BUILD A MOAT

One of my idols, Warren Buffet, frequently talks about how he only invests in businesses with an economic moat, a business with a large competitive advantage that can't easily go away.

There are many different types of economic moats, including companies with high barriers to entry, high switching costs for users, intellectual property (patents, trademarks, etc.), network effects (LinkedIn, Facebook), and many others. These types of businesses should be able to thrive for years and survive short-term hiccups (whether self-inflicted or due to economic downturns) because their profits and market share will be protected due to their unique competitive advantage.

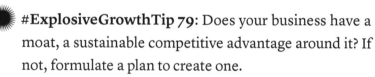 **#ExplosiveGrowthTip 79**: Does your business have a moat, a sustainable competitive advantage around it? If not, formulate a plan to create one.

Although I was enjoying success with The Grade, we still had this looming debt that was creating a lot of pressure on me to shut it down. It was also becoming crystal clear we weren't going to be able to separate The Grade from the larger company, and that was only adding to my misery. I thought to myself, "This is no longer any fun at all." Why was I wasting any more time?

After Tony's program helped me better understand what I was passionate about and why, I was supposed to take massive action right away. That didn't mean I could have waited a few months or years. It meant as soon as the vision struck and I had total clarity, I needed to act on it before it subsided. It also meant that the action had to be very significant in order to create substantial momentum in achieving my goals. In other words, I couldn't just switch to decaf or use an electric toothbrush.

Meanwhile, the pressure of the looming debt due in just months meant I didn't have any freedom to do what I wanted professionally either. I was at someone else's mercy, and that wasn't a fun place to be. Suddenly, it became very clear what I had to do.

I had to sell the company while we still had control of our own destiny.

Two weeks later, I met with a banker who introduced me to Jason Katz, the CEO and founder of Paltalk. It's strange how quickly it all happened, because we had been in discussions for over a year with various potential suitors, but it never worked out. Maybe I just hadn't been ready. Looking back on it now, I think I needed that awakening from the seminar to be ready for my reboot.

The first meeting to discuss a merger took place on March 28, 2016, and we closed the deal on October 7. I knew Paltalk was a great fit right away, because our companies' long-term visions aligned so well. They were also based in New York City (not Silicon Valley), which gave us an instant connection. Beyond that geographical match, they also had a reputation for continuous innovation, which we valued highly. They were a pioneer in the VoIP space by being the first to introduce IM combined with a buddy list, way back in 1999. Paltalk was also a world leader in video chat technology, which made them especially appealing for a merger.

 #ExplosiveGrowthTip 80: If you want more out of life, or have any fears that are holding you back, attend the Tony Robbins event, "Unleash The Power Within."

Book Recommendation: *Unlimited Power* by Tony Robbins.

THE POWER OF VIDEO

Part of the innovator's makeup is to skate to where the

puck is going to be, not to where it is now. In our case, we always believed the puck was going to land in video as the prime method of online communication, including communication on dating sites. Nobody was really sure when, but at some point, some dating app was going to take the puck and masterfully stickhandle their way through a sea of defenders and land in the video space. It was only a matter of time.

We always knew video was going to be the ultimate frontier for online dating, because no other form of communication—email, phone, text, even photos—can give you as much information about someone as five seconds in person (and video is the next best thing).

One big problem with online dating is that people lie too much about things like height, weight, how much hair they have, and other qualities. Photos could be posted from twenty years ago when someone was thirty pounds lighter or had a full head of hair. People can't fake that stuff in a live video chat—it will show the extra weight and the receding hairline. The problem was that people still weren't quite ready to embrace video technology yet.

Andrew had faced a similar dilemma with sixdegrees and digital camera technology many years before. Other dating sites had tried to implement video into their user experience, but for some reason, it just didn't stick. Over the previous year or so, however, things have changed.

Snapchat may be the biggest influencer in taking video sharing to the mainstream public. People aged thirty years and younger have become accustomed to taking videos (rather than photos) of their daily experiences. It's only a matter of time—a very short amount—until dating sites are able to successfully integrate that activity into their user experience.

An additional problem for SNAP was that creating that sort of technology would have been very difficult, costly, and time-consuming. By merging with Paltalk, all that struggle, cost, and development time would be eliminated, as Paltalk already had several very large products that revolved around live video chat experiences—they were already experts.

LET'S MAKE A DEAL

SNAP and Paltalk merged seamlessly with an all-stock transaction in less than six months. As part of the deal, they agreed to pay off our $3 million in debt, which was absolutely critical from our perspective. The new combined company would remain publicly traded under our corporate name, SNAP Interactive.

Paltalk was profitable and more than double our size in terms of revenues, so it only made sense that the share exchange weighed about 77 percent to 23 percent in their favor. In return, I would serve on the board of directors and so would Alex Harrington, my replacement as CEO. Alex would also serve as CEO of the new, combined company.

In the end, it was a straightforward deal, since both companies had a shared vision of a video-enabled future with complementary products.

"SNAPPY" COMPANY NAMES

After the merger, Snapchat filed to go public. While doing so, they also changed their name from Snapchat to Snap, Inc. (whereas our official corporate name was Snap Interactive, Inc.). When Snap, Inc. (formerly Snapchat—see how this can be confusing?), filed for their IPO, our stock surged. This set off a temporary chaos among investors who supposedly confused their newly named company with ours, and our stock skyrocketed from around $4 to $20 per share. Yet again, the media pounced. That confusion became a top story on Bloomberg News, CNBC, Fortune, and several other news sources.

EUROPEAN VACATION II

My first trip to Europe had been so beneficial. It provided

me with so much personal growth, perspective, and appreciation for the subtle and not-so-subtle differences in the various cultures of the world. It had been so good for me, I had promised to go back before I turned thirty. That was a promise I didn't keep, but age is just a number.

Shortly after the merger with Paltalk, I was once again on a plane to Europe, where I spent four weeks talking to a lot of interesting people whom I would have never met if I had remained in my corporate misery. I came home for a week, and then went traveling internationally for another four weeks.

From those two months of trips, I heard so many ideas from different people around the world that I plan on incorporating travel throughout my lifetime, to gain a fresh perspective that will contribute to better business and a better quality of life.

WHAT'S NEXT?

A lot has happened since I first walked out of the doors of Lehman Brothers back in 2005:

- 💣 I've had the undeniable pleasure of working with a lot of outstanding and talented people.
- 💣 I made $78 million in one week.

- I gradually lost nearly all of it over a few years.
- My company was the lead news story in many popular publications and TV shows.
- I've seen a Purple Cow or two.
- I was nominated for Entrepreneur of the Year.
- I rang the opening bell for NASDAQ.
- Did I really turn down Mark Cuban?
- I read a *lot* of books.
- And, I learned a lot of very valuable lessons in business and in life.

Although a lot of lessons were learned on how to launch, build, and optimize products, some of the more important lessons were to not get too deep into the weeds. I learned the importance of focusing on long-term strategy with a constant eye towards creating long-lasting value. More specifically, my experience taught me all about crucial lessons like:

- How to innovate within a larger organization.
- The importance of creating and maintaining an economic moat.
- Having a healthy corporate culture driven by a powerful mission and a shared vision among all employees.
- Recruiting and retaining A-list performers who are a hundred times more valuable than others.

- ☄ The value of a healthy and positive mindset to achieve the ultimate goals.
- ☄ The dangers of accruing debt.
- ☄ The importance of taking money off the table when the opportunity arises.

That last bullet point comes from the end of Chapter 7 when I discussed our first big capital raise, and it should be particularly meaningful for ambitious, young entrepreneurs everywhere.

SNAP Interactive's stock stayed strong long after that deal. It actually doubled in price the following month. A full year later it was still trading at the deal price, which means the company's value was around $80 million. That means I had plenty of time to pocket some earnings from my company's success, but I didn't.

By the time the all-stock merger with Paltalk took place in late 2016, the stock had declined over 97 percent from its high point of $4.50 per share on February 15, 2011. I never sold a single share, which resulted in my paper losses of over $100 million. I urge you to not make the same mistake, and cash out when you can—even if it's just a small percentage.

All is not lost, however, because there's tremendous

opportunity for me on the board of directors at the new company. I'm going to help us achieve next-level success with the invaluable lessons I've learned from my experience, detailed throughout these pages.

Starting a new business, watching it grow through innovation and hard work, and impacting people's lives for the better has always been my passion. Worrying about debt payment and having investors control my destiny has never been appealing to me. Now, I have the freedom and the fresh perspective I need to create something special once again.

Soon enough, I will be taking those eleven years of knowledge and experience to lead another company to hopefully even greater heights. In the meantime, you can probably find me tinkering with innovation and searching for how to do things better in my new garage, while also keeping a sharp eye out for the next Purple Cow.

Access more *Explosive Growth* materials at http://www.explosive-growth.com

Social: @ExplosiveGrowthCEO, @CliffLerner, #ExplosiveGrowthTip

APPENDIX

MORE LESSONS LEARNED AND ADVICE ON ACQUISITIONS FROM JASON KATZ, FOUNDER AND CEO OF PALTALK

Before cable, DSL, and Wi-Fi, we connected to the internet by using an archaic technology called dial-up, via 28.8K modems. In 1998, cell phones were still primarily used for actually talking to people, texting didn't exist, and Snapchat was a long time away. AOL Instant Messaging (IM) was one of the very few instant messengers available, certainly the only one most people even knew about. I saw value in IM right away, however. Early on, I was convinced that IM was a technology that was going to be in everyone's future.

My aha moment, which inspired the creation of Paltalk, came when I was using IM to plan a ski trip with a friend. My then two-year-old son decided to do what toddlers typically do (whatever the heck they feel like), and jumped on me, preventing me from using my hands to type. That's when I thought, "Why can't I do this with audio instead of typing?"

At the time, nobody had an instant messenger application where the default action was to talk instead of type, and that's when I created AVM Software dba Paltalk. I funded the company myself for a year, found some talented developers, and launched in January 1999 as free software on CNET.com and other similar sites.

People liked that first version of the software and it spread virally, because it was a quality build, and it enabled people to speak to each other worldwide for free. Then came the dotcom bubble-burst of 2001. Later on, in 2008, the country experienced the mortgage-driven financial crisis. Unlike many technology companies, however, we survived both of those economic meltdowns. Why? Because we made money.

LESSONS LEARNED

The Importance of Cash Flow. The failed dotcoms of

2001 were pre-pay-per-click ad-based companies. We put a subscription element into our software that provided a free download, free talk, and free broadcast of video, but we charged for viewing other people's videos, a Freemium model we have retained ever since. Cash flow was coming in and we were fully independent. We raised a fair amount of venture capital as well, but as long as the software was working, it didn't matter what the world was doing, because we made money on our own.

Localize. Another important lesson that I stress to anyone developing software is that as Americans, we tend to foolishly think that everyone around the world speaks English. They don't. In fact, most websites cite just over 90 percent of the world speaks a language other than English as their native tongue. That astonishes a lot of Americans, but it's true. With that knowledge in hand, localization of your software presents gigantic opportunities, especially in the Far East where there are large populations of people in developed countries like India and China. I learned this very valuable lesson more than a few years ago, and it rewarded me with tremendous growth ever since.

Push the Pedal to the Metal. I spoke at a conference called Voice on the Net (VON) many years ago, and I got a question from the audience, asking me what I thought of Skype. I basically dismissed the question as irrelevant.

That was a mistake, and I paid for it. At the time, Skype had just launched, and to my detriment, I had never heard of it.

What do most people think Skype did? Most people think it enabled people to talk to each other for free over the internet.

What did Skype really do? Skype enabled people worldwide to avoid costly long distance calling by using the internet to carry people's voices.

I was already providing free talk, but unlike the United States, the rest of the world didn't have free or very low-cost long-distance plans, so they took to Skype because of that nuance that I overlooked, which also speaks to the necessity for localization in more ways than just language. Don't be dismissive of anything even remotely relevant to your industry. Looking back, I should have pressed on the gas a little harder, but that wasn't easy to do in those days. It seemed like the world was collapsing around us, and we felt good because we could at least control our one destiny. Even still, I could have probably pushed a little harder.

ADVICE ON ACQUISITIONS

Most businesses experience an initial burst of growth

when they first launch. The hard part comes after the business runs through all that influx of activity. The next thing to do is to acquire growth, which is why I bought a half-dozen companies or more over the years.

The Continuing Importance of Cash Flow. Companies can do different things to make them look more interesting and suitable for acquisition. Cash flow is probably the best way to do it. A company with good cash flow is like buying a blue-chip stock. However, If I buy a company that isn't making revenue, then I better be prepared for a long-term investment, and I better be right on with my assumption that the ROI will eventually be there.

Low Risk/High Reward. Another way to become attractive for acquisition is if the company has very little expense, or if it's a product that works well and is expandable. In other words, there's a small investment with upside. For example, I bought a company called Vumber, which had revenue of only $7,500 per month, but I only paid around $100,000 for it. Now, it earns about $60,000 per month, so in that case, buying something with upside at a cheap cost worked out very well.

Barter for Legal Work. There are going to be significant legal expenses when a company is going through a merger and acquisition (M&A). In the early days, I was fortunate, because I had a lawyer's education, so I knew that starting and running my own company was going to incur a lot of legal expenses. The problem was that I didn't have a lot of money to pay lawyers every time I needed legal work performed. So, I went to a law firm and offered them a small amount of equity in exchange for legal services. Secondly, when M&A is about to happen, the law firm should agree to a cap on legal fees for the acquisition. This is a huge way for start-ups to save money when it is at its most precarious level of need.

REASONS FOR MY BIGGEST ACQUISITIONS

HearMe was my first acquisition, and it was an asset purchase. It ended up generating good revenue, but that's not why I bought it. I bought it because I believed it represented innovative and novel intellectual property for pennies on the dollar. The key to the acquisition was the time frame, which was during the dot-com bubble burst of December 2001. We were willing to pay cash for the assets at a time when seemingly nobody else was. HearMe was a victim of the dot-com collapse, and they were liquidating. Therefore, we were clearly the beneficiary of being able to acquire uniquely amazing assets that required hundreds of millions of dollars in venture capital to produce.

Camfrog was the second big acquisition I made. That one

was a no-brainer, because it had no marketing expenses at all—still doesn't—and it still generated revenue. They had cash flow, which as I mentioned, is something I always look for with an acquisition.

One of the interesting things that happened with this merger was they were selling lifetime subscriptions when we took over, but I'm not crazy about that, because I want the money to keep coming in, year after year. It's hard to sell renewals if the user base has a lifetime subscription. We stopped those after the merger, which the user base didn't love, but we grandfathered the current users, which made the change more palatable.

Vumber was strictly a deal for technology, which allows users to put a different phone number on a cell phone without getting a different SIM card. Hence, the term Vumber or virtual number. I liked that technology right away because I saw a purpose. A business might be in the 212 area code, but want a 213 number because they want to be in California. Socially, I thought it might be a good way for people to protect their privacy. Especially for dating, someone might want a dedicated number just for dating purposes, so they don't have to give away their real number to people they don't know well enough yet.

Snap Interactive provided us with an opportunity to

create liquidity for the Paltalk shareholders since they are publicly traded. There's also substantial upside for the shareholders as the newly formed company executes on our business plan. While Paltalk was performing well in making money, distributing dividends, and being in the market for a long time, there was no real ready market for the shares, until now. However, the primary reason for the merger was it involved two technology pioneers and innovators in their respective industries. They are just a few blocks from each other in NYC, and have a shared vision for a video-enabled future, and massive complementary platforms with proprietary live-video technology—that's a winning formula.

ABOUT THE AUTHOR

CLIFF LERNER is an accomplished business leader who gave up a lucrative Wall Street career to launch an online dating start-up. With little funding, Cliff founded Snap Interactive. His start-up would go on to create the first successful Facebook dating app, grow revenues 4,412 percent in five years, and sign up more than 100 million users. Cliff resides in New York City and is always on the lookout for his next entrepreneurial endeavor.

Made in the USA
Middletown, DE
18 January 2019